PENC

ASK THE MONK

Nityanand Charan Das is a practising monk at the Sri Sri Radha Gopinath Temple—ISKCON Chowpatty—in Mumbai, and a visionary who wishes to revolutionize the current urban scenario by aiding people in leading a life of purpose, fulfilment and satisfaction. He also specializes in guiding today's youth, including children and teenagers, to reconnect with their roots and lead a simple yet happy life.

He first connected with ISKCON when he was twenty-one years old and in college. He joined as a full-time monk at twenty-four, after completing his engineering degree. He focuses on leading a balanced life wherein one should think of advancing not only materially but spiritually as well.

He specializes in simplifying sacred teachings, so they resonate with anyone and everyone, and his message is simple:

'Spiritual life is not a life of rejection. It is a life of connection.'

We do not have to give up anything, we simply have to add this valuable dimension to our lives.

Complementing this, he facilitates trips to sacred destinations, conducting retreats to provide practical experiences of spirituality. His divine radiance can be felt far and wide—his lectures are heard in every major city of India and in more than fifty countries across the globe. He is also the author of the national bestseller *Icons of Grace: Twenty-One Lives That Defined Indian Spirituality* and *Bound by Love*.

Ask the MONK

Answers *to* Life's Most Intriguing Questions

NITYANAND CHARAN DAS

Bestselling author of ICONS OF GRACE:
TWENTY-ONE LIVES THAT DEFINED INDIAN SPIRITUALITY

PENGUIN
ANANDA

An imprint of Penguin Random House

PENGUIN ANANDA

USA | Canada | UK | Ireland | Australia
New Zealand | India | South Africa | China

Penguin Ananda is part of the Penguin Random House group of companies
whose addresses can be found at global.penguinrandomhouse.com

Published by Penguin Random House India Pvt. Ltd
4th Floor, Capital Tower 1, MG Road,
Gurugram 122 002, Haryana, India

First published in Penguin Ananda by Penguin Random House India 2022

ISBN 9780143459026

Typeset in Adobe Garamond Pro by Manipal Technologies Limited, Manipal
Printed at Thomson Press India Ltd, New Delhi

www.penguin.co.in

To Brahma-Madhva-Gaudiya-Guru-Shishya Parampara,
who, through their deep knowledge and cutting logic, removed
the veil of illusion and brought immense clarity to our
thought process

Contents

Introduction   xiii

Q. 1   Is everything predestined? Do sciences such as
       palmistry, astrology and numerology help?   1

Q. 2   Why is Lord Krishna/God blue/green?   5

Q. 3   What is the relationship between Lord Krishna
       and Lord Shiva?   7

Q. 4   Why should we worry about any future life
       apart from this life?   11

Q. 5   Does Vedic literature allow meat-eating?   14

Q. 6   If we avoid meat because we don't want to
       cause violence, then doesn't eating vegetables
       also involve violence?   22

Q. 7   What is the size of the soul?   25

Q. 8   Is God formless or does He have a form?   28

Q. 9   If God is everywhere, do we need to go to
       a temple?   33

Q. 10 How should one pray?   35

Q. 11 Why don't we remember our past lives?   39

Q. 12 Who is the supreme: Lord Vishnu or Lord
       Krishna?   42

Q. 13 Why did Lord Krishna have 16,108 wives?   50

Q. 14 Why did Lord Krishna engage in the Raas Lila,
       dancing with the gopis in the middle of
       the night?   52

Q. 15 In the Ramayana, why did Lord Rama kill
       Vali from behind a tree?   56

Q. 16 What happens after death?   60

Q. 17 Why do bad things happen to good people?   63

Q. 18 How can we control our jealousy and ego?   65

Q. 19 Can I be spiritual without being religious?   67

Q. 20 Why did Lord Krishna not marry Radharani?   69

Q. 21 Do all paths lead to the same goal?   72

Q. 22 Did Lord Rama eat meat?   76

Q. 23 The Vedas say 'na tasya pratima asti'
       (You are not a *pratima* or a *moorti* [idol]).
       Why then do we worship idols?   79

Q. 24 Is lying sinful? How can we give it up?   82

Q. 25 Why did Yudhishthir gamble? Wasn't he at fault
       for engaging in it and then losing everything?   84

Q. 26 If Lord Krishna is God, then how could a
       hunter's arrow have killed Him?   87

Q. 27 Isn't fasting an unnecessary form of self-torture?   91

Q. 28 Why did Lord Rama banish Sita? 93

Q. 29 What is the purpose of life? 97

Q. 30 How can we experience spiritual bliss? 100

Q. 31 What is the significance of the aarti performed
in temples? 102

Q. 32 Why do we offer food to God? 105

Q. 33 Is there any scientific proof for the existence
of the soul? 109

Q. 34 Why do people fight in the name of religion? 112

Q. 35 If God has designed our world, then why is
there so much suffering here? 117

Q. 36 What is the role of logic on the spiritual path? 120

Q. 37 When God is one, why does the Vedic
tradition teach the worship of many gods? 123

Q. 38 Why do you consider Krishna to be God? 127

Q. 39 Doesn't spirituality demand blind faith? 133

Q. 40 Even though Ravana kidnapped Sita, he never
used force on her. Was he not a gentleman then? 136

Q. 41 Is the law of karma scientific? 139

Q. 42 What is the need for rituals? Is it not enough
to just think of God? 141

Q. 43 If God exists, why can't we see Him? 145

Q. 44 Is there any proof of reincarnation? 150

Q. 45 Aren't yajnas, in which grains and
ghee are poured into a fire, a foolish
waste of money? 153

Q. 46 Can spirituality free one from stress and fear?   157

Q. 47 How is a holy place different from any
       other place?   160

Q. 48 What is the significance of Diwali?   162

Q. 49 Is forgiveness possible, especially towards
       someone who repeatedly hurts us?   165

Q. 50 Why does the Bhagavad Gita recommend
       working with detachment?   168

Q. 51 Why do natural calamities occur?   171

Q. 52 Why do we not get action-reaction (karma)
       in the same life?   174

Q. 53 Why are the ignorant not excused by the law
       of karma?   177

Q. 54 Why do natural calamities kill thousands of
       innocent people?   180

Q. 55 Why does the Bhagavad Gita call for
       violence?   182

Q. 56 Isn't being good and doing good to others
       enough? I live honestly and do not harm
       others. Why do I need God?'   186

Q. 57 Why do people commit suicide?   190

Q. 58 Is work worship?   193

Q. 59 Is seeing believing? In the present scientific
       age, why should we believe in anything
       spiritual, especially in a God that cannot
       be seen?   196

Q. 60 Can we be spiritual, but not religious?   201

Q. 61 Which is the best, easiest and most practical
form of spiritual practice in today's day and age? 204

Q. 62 Was Arjuna's killing of Karna, when the latter
was chariot-less, unfair and against the
Kshatriya codes? 208

Q. 63 Why did Bhima kill Duryodhana unfairly by
hitting him below the waist during their final
battle in the Mahabharata war? 211

Q. 64 If God created everything, who created God? 213

Q. 65 Who is a guru? How do we find him? 215

Q. 66 Are the Gods of different religions different? 220

Q. 67 Why should we spend on temples when we
can serve poor people or open hospitals? 222

Q. 68 Are the scriptures valid? 227

Q. 69 Why was Ekalavya treated so unfairly? 231

Q. 70 What decides the future of a special/intellectually
disabled child since he cannot perform any karma? 234

Q. 71 Are dreams real or not? 236

Q. 72 Why do we shave our heads at Tirupati Balaji? 238

Q. 73 Why do spiritualists recommend food without
onion and garlic? 241

Q. 74 Does Lord Shiva smoke or consume
marijuana/weed? 244

Last Words 247
Bibliography 249
Acknowledgements 253

Introduction

I keep six honest serving-men
(They taught me all I knew);
Their names are What and Why and When
And How and Where and Who.
—Rudyard Kipling

Asking questions is a sign of intelligence.

The power of asking questions in both our work and personal lives cannot be overstated and impacts every area of our lives. In fact, in hindsight, we can observe that every learning we have had has been brought about by us asking questions.

During our childhood, questions and curiosity are a natural part of our interactions with the world around us. There is always a wondering 'why' and an inquisitive 'how', much to the bewilderment of the adults. Over time, as we grow older, we become less and less curious. Society drills it into our minds that giving answers is more important, be it when giving exams, in interviews or to contribute to a conversation. As adults, we eventually stop asking questions, and conform by falling into a routine.

Children seldom hesitate before asking us 'why' countless times until they're satisfied with innocent wonderment, to understand the world around them.

Simply imbibing this one quality from them, applying the same sense of critical questioning to our lives, has the power to transform, to revolutionize our lives. Defining our 'why' is of utmost importance. If we do not ask 'why' over and over again, we will never succeed at the 'what'.

The Vedic scriptures, guidebooks for humanity, encourage us to question things, right from the very beginning of our human lives.

But what type of questions should we ask?

The Vedanta Sutra (1.1.1) answers:

athato brahma jigyasa

'[Since you have got this human life] Now is the time to enquire about the absolute truth.'

Enquiring merely about our basic physiological needs of eating, sleeping, relaxing, etc. is not something extraordinary. Even animals do that. A bird wakes up early in the morning and starts questioning, 'Where is the food?'

The special ability to make higher enquiries is what truly separates us from the other species.

It therefore becomes our moral duty to ask questions beyond our basic needs; questions such as:

'Who am I?'
'Where do I come from?'
'Where will I go?'
'What is the purpose of life?'
'Who is God?'
'What is my relationship with Him?'
'How do I revive that relationship?'
'Why do I suffer even if I do not want to?'

And so on.

The following Vedic verse confirms the same:

ahara nidra bhaya maithunam ca
samanyam etat pasubhir naranam
dharmo hi tesam adhika viseso
dharmena hinah pasubhih samana

'Both animals and humans share the activities of eating,
sleeping, mating and defending. But the special property
of humans is that they can engage in spiritual life.
Therefore, without spiritual life, humans are on the level
of animals.' [Hitopadesa 25]

And thus, this book.

Ask the Monk is a practising monk's humble attempt to answer over seventy typical questions of a higher nature, which are crucial to embark on the journey of self-discovery and self-realization.

I have, over the years, been asked these questions by a nine-year-old and an eighty-year-old as well. Thus, this book is for children, teenagers, the young, the middle-aged, millennials, Gen-Zs or any lost soul looking to be found.

The book tries to address the confusion and doubts arising from common misconceptions, controversial references in scriptures such as the Mahabharata and Ramayana, and various other subjects ranging from rituals, destiny and karma to the mind and anything else that keeps us from truth, impeding our progress.

To accomplish this, we have taken the help of all three aspects necessary to prove a point; it is the intersection of science, logic and scriptures.

We hope that this book helps sincere readers on their journey to discover the self and discover this world, provides much sought-after clarity on various important issues and destroys the demons of doubt in the reader's mind.

Because if we do not destroy them, they will end up destroying us.

Happy reading, and keep questioning!

Q. 1

Is everything predestined? Do sciences such as palmistry, astrology and numerology help?

People get very excited about knowing their future. Vedic sciences such as palmistry, numerology and astrology fuel excitement by predicting what is in store for one. These predictions can bring happiness, but also distress if they are not what we expect or desire. This can either make us too hopeful or it can make us feel hopeless because we tend to resign ourselves to what has been predicted. However, we have news!

We are not programmed robots! We are human beings blessed with the ability to make choices.

If everything is pre-written, then why work at all? We always have free will, something even God Himself will never interfere in. What happens to us is destiny, but how we respond to it is entirely our choice, and by our choices we can brighten or darken our future.

Essentially, any method of learning about the future is like a weather forecast. The weather forecast might say that it will rain tomorrow, but we decide if we want to get drenched. And even if we do decide to go out, we can always equip ourselves with an umbrella or a raincoat and thus avoid getting wet.

The various branches of Vedic knowledge that are concerned with knowing about the future are based on an understanding that there are signs of the future that are present either in our bodily characteristics or in the planetary alignments at the moment of our birth, or the date of birth and time. But these are just signs and not compulsions. Any form of prediction can primarily determine what might happen to us, but it doesn't determine our response. So, destiny essentially refers to 'what happens to us', and free will essentially refers to 'how we respond to it'.

Even astrologers, numerologists or palmists give remedies such as wearing certain stones or performing certain rituals. This goes to show that even they believe things can be changed by taking the proper steps. Now whether we come across a genuine practitioner is a matter of good luck, but the point is that things can change.

Of course, destiny is strong, and its influence might still give us the urge to go out when it rains despite knowing the weather forecast, but again, we do have the choice to resist the temptation. The ultimate choice lies with us, and we can always choose to act in a way that is for our personal growth. That ability becomes more and more pronounced when we have the right association, especially with those who are spiritually advanced.

Lord Brahma tells us in the Brahma Samhita (5.27):

karmani nirdahati kintu cha bhakti-bhajam
govindam adi-purusham tam aham bhajami

'I adore the primeval Lord Govinda, who burns up to their
roots, all karmas of those who are imbued with devotion.'

Lord Krishna Himself says in the Bhagavad Gita (18.66):

sarva-dharman parityajy
mam ekam saranam vraja
aham tvam sarva-papebhyo
moksayisyami ma sucah

'Abandon all varieties of religion and just surrender
unto Me. I shall deliver you from all sinful reactions.
Do not fear.'

A person who commits a serious crime and is punished by
the law can still be pardoned by the king or the president of
a country if they see a genuine reason to do so. If a human
being can have such authority, why do we think the Supreme
Lord cannot pardon us if we sincerely repent and choose to
rectify our wrong behaviour?

Anyone who engages in the devotional service of the
Lord can have their destiny changed at any time. We cannot
change it, but through our choices, we can attract His grace
and He can do it for us.

So the best choice is to engage in devotional practices,
beginning with the chanting of the holy names of the Lord

(Hare Krishna Hare Krishna Krishna Krishna Hare Hare, Hare Rama Hare Rama Rama Rama Hare Hare) and hearing from scriptures such as the Bhagavad Gita and Srimad Bhagavatam on a regular basis. These practices can sharpen our intellect and thus help us make the right decisions in life.

If our lives were just unchangeable scripts, then there would be no point in God giving us scriptures and sending spiritual masters and saints into this world to guide us about the do's and don'ts. The very fact that Krishna, in the Bhagavad Gita, talks about various choices and their consequences and then says, 'Now do as you like,' proves that after knowing everything, the ultimate choice lies with us.

Palmistry, numerology and astrology, as brilliant as they are, have their limitations. Srila Prabhupada, the Founder Acharya of ISKCON, stated that if we just clap our hands in the kirtan of the Lord's holy names, then all the lines of our hands will change. Thus, by the sincere practice of devotional service beginning with hearing and chanting (as mentioned above), destiny can certainly take a U-turn for the better. Every moment is a choice, and every choice can bring a drastic change.

Q. 2

Why is Lord Krishna/God blue/green?

Lord Krishna is blue because He is a person, and every person is allowed to have choices; He wants to be blue. And, thus, He is blue.

When He descends in various incarnations, He assumes different colours. Srimad Bhagavatam mentions Krishna appearing as a boar with whitish and reddish complexions in two different millenniums, as Lord Rama having a green complexion, and as Chaitanya Mahaprabhu with a golden complexion. So it is the Lord's choice as to which colour He wishes to appear in just as we can choose to wear different coloured garments for different occasions as per our desire. In fact, the first aphorism of the Vedanta Sutra explains, '*janmady asya yatah*'—the Supreme Lord is the one from whom everything emanates—which implies that the wide spectrum of independent tastes that we have actually come from the Lord being the supreme father, since the children must have the qualities of the father. Since He has choices, so do we, being His parts and parcels.

We can't apply logic to someone's individuality and certainly not to God's. Even in this world, everything cannot be explained logically.

The Vedanta Sutra *(1.1.3)* explains: *Sastrayonitvat* (शास्त्रयोनित्वात्). This means that God can be known only through scripture and not through inference or logic. We depend on revelation.

Someone who is beyond the realm of logic cannot be brought into the realm of logic just because we like logic. We should not reduce reality to fit into our understanding. Rather we should expand our understanding so that we can grasp reality.

Logic is like a tool having a utility. But just like any other tool, it has limitations. When it comes to matters such as God's personality, personal features, attributes etc., then logic or rational thinking is not enough. For that we need revelation, which means that we need to learn from the scriptures and apply what we learn to evolve in our understanding.

Q. 3

What is the relationship between Lord Krishna and Lord Shiva?

Lord Shiva and Lord Krishna are one and yet different. Lord Brahma gives a beautiful analogy to explain this in the Brahma Samhita (5.45) (prayers offered by him at the beginning of creation after having the absolute truth revealed to him):

kshiram yatha dadhi vikara-vishesha-yogat
sanjayate na hi tatah prithag asti hetoho
yah shambhutam api tatha samupaiti karyad
govindam adi-purusham tam aham bhajami

'Just as milk is transformed into curd by the action of
acids, but yet the effect (curd) is neither the same as nor
different from its cause (milk), so I adore the primeval
Lord Govinda of whom the state of Sambhu (Shiva)
is a transformation for the performance of the work of
destruction.'

Curd is nothing but the transformed form of milk in touch with acids, but at the same time, milk is the source of curd. Lord Krishna is like milk and Lord Shiva is curd. Lord Krishna is pure spirit. When He comes in contact with material creation, He manifests Himself into a different *tattva* (category) called Shiva Tattva. But just as we cannot get the same benefits from curd as from milk, similarly, the worship of Lord Shiva won't yield the same benefits as the worship of Lord Krishna.

Thus, Lord Shiva is one of the expansions of Lord Krishna for the specific purpose of destruction. In other words, when Lord Krishna's destructive power takes a form, He is known as Lord Shiva.

However, Lord Shiva is a very mysterious personality and plays different roles in creation.

He plays the role of demigod too but is not a demigod as Lord Brahma or Lord Indra (the king of heavens). He is above all of them, but he is also not worshipped nor does he like to be worshiped as God. He takes great pleasure in being addressed as a devotee of the Supreme Lord.

As mentioned in the greatest scripture Srimad Bhagavatam (12.13.16):

nimna-ganam yatha ganga
devanam achyuto yatha
vaishnavanam yatha shambhuh
purananam idam tatha

'Just as the Ganga is the greatest of all rivers, Lord Achyuta [Krishna] the supreme among deities and Lord

Sambhu [Shiva] the greatest of Vaishnavas, so Shrimad
Bhagavatam is the greatest of all Puranas.'

Further Lord Shiva himself says in Srimad Bhagavatam
(4.24.28):

> yah param ramhasah sakshat
> tri-gunaj jiva-samjnitat
> bhagavantam vasudevam
> prapannah sa priyo hi me

'Any person who is surrendered to the Supreme
Personality of Godhead, Krishna, the controller of
everything—material nature as well as the living entity—
is actually very dear to me.'

Lord Shiva awards material opulence to His worshippers. But
to the ones He is especially pleased with, to those who have
a pure heart and do not desire anything material from Him,
He gives what is closest to His heart. And that is devotional
service to Lord Krishna. He brings such people into the realm
of service to Lord Krishna.

Vallabhacharya was a great devotee of both Lord Krishna
and Lord Shiva. Once, distressed with the ups and downs of
life, he went to a temple of Lord Shiva and started praying
fervently. Touched by his prayers, Lord Shiva appeared and
asked him his wish. Vallabhacharya was surprised, but since
he was a pure-hearted devotee, instead of asking Lord Shiva
to fulfil a material desire, he said, 'Please give me what is most

dear to You.' Lord Shiva smiled broadly and gave him a deity of Lord Krishna. Since then, Vallabhacharya worshipped Lord Krishna, but never rejected Lord Shiva. In fact, he considered Lord Shiva his guru.

And so, Lord Shiva and Lord Krishna are one and yet different. They are one in the sense that they are the manifestation of the same absolute truth, but for different functions.

However, whoever we are worshipping, as per our faith, we can pray to them to give us whatever they think is best and closest to their heart and just like Vallabhacharya, we will be guided to the best even if we do not know who or what that best is.

Q. 4

Why should we worry about any future life apart from this life?

This is not our only life and one day we will have to leave this world even if we do not wish to. And our future life will depend on our actions in this life.

Life is not a one-day match but a multi-innings test match. And the next innings will depend on how well or badly we played in this one. We begin from where we left off. So, to avoid any future distress and have a better future life, we need to think about it in this life.

And spirituality apart, don't we follow this system in our daily life as well? Don't we worry about our children's future welfare and thus send them to the best of schools and encourage them to work hard to have a better career? Don't we make investments to make our future secure, especially anticipating any emergency that might pop up? These are called short-term investments, and our holy scriptures, which are the guidebooks for humanity, encourage us to make long-term investments as life continues even beyond the present body.

As Lord Krishna says in the Bhagavad Gita (2.13):

> *dehino 'smin yatha dehe*
> *kaumaram yauvanam jara*
> *tatha dehantara-praptir*
> *dhiras tatra na muhyati*

'As the embodied soul continually passes in this body,
from boyhood to youth to old age, the soul similarly
passes into another body at death. The self-realized soul
is not bewildered by such a change.'

Further He says in the Bhagavad Gita (2.27):

> *jatasya hi dhruvo mrityur*
> *dhruvam janma mritasya ca*
> *tasmad apariharye 'rthe*
> *na tvam sochitum arhasi*

'For one who has taken his birth, death is certain; and
for one who is dead, birth is certain. Therefore, in the
unavoidable discharge of your duty, you should not
lament.'

Thus, we must recognize that we are eternal beings and our
life will not end with death, but will continue, and therefore
we must prepare for the future. There is strong scientific
evidence of reincarnation through the recollection of past life
memories by children as investigated by Dr Ian Stevenson

(around 3000 cases) in different parts of the world. Thus, science and scripture both confirm that we will have life after this life, and therefore it is wise to prepare for it. Just like a child who knows there will be exams after six months, we must be sensible enough to prepare for the same, to take responsibility for our lives.

Q. 5

Does Vedic literature allow meat-eating?

A small yes and a big NO.

Let us understand this.

Vedic literature is not exclusive but inclusive: there is not just one way for people, but multiple ways depending on the evolution of their consciousness, and the ultimate goal of the Vedas remains to gradually uplift everyone from whatever level they are on to the highest goal of life, i.e., to realize who we are, who God is and how to serve Him with love.

Prominently, Vedic literature highly recommends vegetarianism, and the reference to non-vegetarianism is negligible.

Let us consider the following Vedic quotes that disapprove of, even denounce, meat-eating.

Manu Samhita (the law book for humankind)

'Meat can never be obtained without injury to living creatures, and injury to sentient beings is detrimental to the attainment of heavenly bliss; let him therefore shun the use of meat. Having well considered the disgusting origin of flesh and the cruelty of fettering and slaying corporeal beings, let him entirely abstain from eating flesh.' (Manu Samhita 5.48-49)

'He who permits the slaughter of an animal, he who cuts it up, he who kills it, he who buys or sells meat, he who cooks it, he who serves it up, and he who eats it, must all be considered as the slayers of the animal. There is no greater sinner than that man who though not worshiping the gods or the ancestors, seeks to increase the bulk of his own flesh by the flesh of other beings.' (Manu Samhita 5.51-52)

'If he has a strong desire [for meat] he may make an animal of clarified butter or one of flour [and eat that]; but let him never seek to destroy an animal without a [lawful] reason. As many hairs as the slain beast has, so often indeed will he who killed it without a [lawful] reason suffer a violent death in future births.' (Manu Samhita 5.37-38)

'He who injures harmless creatures from a wish to give himself pleasure, never finds happiness in this life or the next.' (Manu Samhita 5.45)

'By subsisting on pure fruits and roots, and by eating food fit for ascetics in the forest, one does not gain so great a reward as by entirely avoiding the use of flesh.' (Manu Samhita 5.54-55)

'By not killing any living being, one becomes fit for salvation.' (Manu Samhita 6.60)

Mahabharata

'He who desires to augment his own flesh by eating the flesh of other creatures, lives in misery in whatever species he may take his [next] birth.' (Mahabharata, Anu.115.47)

'The purchaser of flesh performs violence by his wealth; he who eats flesh does so by enjoying its taste; the killer does violence by actually tying and killing the animal. Thus, there are three forms of killing. He who brings flesh or sends for it, he who cuts off the limbs of an animal, and he who purchases, sells, or cooks flesh and eats it—all these are to be considered meat-eaters.' (Mahabharata, Anu.115.40)

'The sins generated by violence curtail the life of the perpetrator. Therefore, even those who are anxious for their own welfare should abstain from meat-eating.' (Mahabharata, Anu.115.33)

'The virtuous Narada has said that that man who wishes to multiply his own flesh by eating the flesh of other creatures meets with disaster.' (Mahabharata, Anu.115.9-12)

'What necessity be said of those innocent and healthy creatures gifted with love of life, when they are sought to be killed by sinful wretches living by slaughter? Therefore, O King, know that the discarding of meat is the highest refuge of religion, of the celestial region, and of happiness. Abstention of injury [to others] is the highest religion. It is, again, the highest penance. It is also the highest truth from which all duty emanates.' (Mahabharata, Anu.115.21-23)

'Flesh cannot be had from grass or wood or stone. Unless a living creature is killed, it cannot be procured. Hence is the fault of eating flesh. Those persons who are for satisfying the sensation of taste, should be known as Rakshasas [flesh-eating demons] pervaded by the quality of Darkness.' (Mahabharata, Anu.115.24-25)

'If there were nobody who ate flesh, then there would be nobody to slay living creatures. The man who slays living creatures kills them for the sake of the person who eats flesh. If flesh were not considered as food, there would then be no destruction of living creatures. It is for the sake of the eater that the destruction of living entities is carried on in the world. Since, O you of great splendour, the period of life is shortened by persons who kill living creatures or cause them to be killed, it is clear that the person who seeks his own good should give up meat altogether. Those dreadful persons who are engaged in the destruction of living beings never find protectors when they are in need. Such persons should always be severely punished even as a beast of prey.' (Mahabharata, Anu.115.29-32)

'Listen to me, O king of kings, as I tell you this, O sinless one, there is absolute happiness in abstaining from meat, O king. He who practises severe austerities for a century, and he who abstains from meat, are both equally meritorious. This is my opinion. (Mahabharata, Anu.115.52-53)

'Yudhisthira said: Alas, those cruel men who, not caring for various other sorts of food, want only flesh, are really like great Rakshasas [meat-eating demons].' (Mahabharata, Anu.116.1)

'Bhishma said: That man who wishes to increase his own flesh by the meat of another living creature is such that there is none meaner and crueller than he. In this world there is nothing that is dearer to a creature than his life. Hence, one should show mercy to the lives of others as he does to his own life. Forsooth, O son, flesh has its origin in the vital seed. There is great sin attached to its eating, as, indeed, there is merit in abstaining from it.' (Mahabharata, Anu.116.11-13)

'Hence a person of purified soul should be merciful to all living creatures. That man, O king, who abstains from every kind of meat from his birth, acquires a large space in the celestial region. They who eat the flesh of animals who are desirous of life, are themselves [later] eaten by the animals they eat. This is my opinion. Since he has eaten me, I shall eat him in return. This, O Bharata, forms the character as Mamsah [meaning flesh] of Mamsah [me, he will eat for having eaten him]. The destroyer is always slain. After him the eater meets with the same fate.' (Mahabharata, Anu.116.32-35)

Bhagavata Purana

'Those who are ignorant of real dharma and, though wicked and haughty, account themselves virtuous, kill animals without any feeling of remorse or fear of punishment. Further, in their next lives, such sinful persons will be eaten by the same creatures they have killed in this world.' (Bhagavata Purana 11.5.14)

Thus we see that Vedic literature vehemently condemns meat-eating.

Then what about the references to eating meat?

These references are not recommendations. They are concessions.

Nonetheless, these references do exist. Some people who want to justify their meat-eating habits may seek out references that allow meat-eating. But if we look at those references, practically all of them are in the context of yagya or sacrifice. It is conditional.

So why does Vedic literature allow meat-eating in certain instances?

Vedic literature does not offer spirituality in only one form. It recognizes that different people are at different levels of evolution or capacity to practise spiritual life. And based on their individual capacities, they can follow recommendations at different levels. That is why for those who are addicted to meat-eating, it is allowed under certain restricted circumstances. So, these statements in the scriptures are concessions, not recommendations.

What is the difference between a concession and a recommendation? If a patient is diagnosed with diabetes, the doctor tells him to take a particular medicine and avoid all sugar. This is the recommendation. But say the patient says, 'I can't live without sugar. I must have sugar.' So the doctor says, 'Okay, you can have sugar. Eat one sweet, but only once a week.' This is a concession. But the patient announces that the doctor has instructed him to eat sweets, even though this was not an instruction or recommendation, but a concession. Concession means that which is not necessarily good for one is allowed only because one wants it.

So Vedic literature recommends vegetarianism, but the concession is that you can be non-vegetarian under certain circumstances. What are those circumstances? If we perform yagya on certain holy days in which an animal is sacrificed and then offered to Goddess Kali or some other devi or *devata*, then that meat is consumed. These holy days do not occur very often. The ultimate purpose is to discourage cruelty. But to those who will not move ahead in life unless something they want is given to them, the scriptures say, 'All right! We are not denying you your right to eat. You can certainly eat on these days.' Just as the doctor's purpose is to restrict the eating of sugar, even though he would prefer that you did not take sugar at all.

When sacrifices are offered to the Goddess Kali, she doesn't eat them as she is a vaishnavi and wife of Lord Shiva, the most compassionate personality. But because the worshippers desire the meat, sacrifices were started to regulate their desires.

But even such sacrifices were stopped by the acharyas or spiritual masters such as Madhvacharya, Ramanujacharya and others who later appeared to systematize and revive Vedic culture. Today, all over the world, people are recognizing the value of vegetarianism because of the ecological problems created by eating meat. So rather than seeking out obscure verses in Vedic literature to justify one's meat-eating, let us recognize the Vedic tradition and its acclaimed vegetarianism. This tradition is now setting an example for the rest of the world where the vegetarian alternative is not just an alternative but a necessity for the survival of our planet and for the survival of humanity.

When we quote Vedic literature, we must look into our own hearts and ask whether we are quoting it just to validate what we are doing or to actually learn about the essential principles. Recommendations are many, but concessions are few. So, what is our focus? Recommendation or concession?

Q. 6

If we avoid meat because we don't want to cause violence, then doesn't eating vegetables also involve violence?

The Vedic scriptures state, '*jivo jivasya jivanam*' (Srimad Bhagavatam 1.13.47), which means that one living being is food for another. So each living entity has to subsist on another. We cannot avoid violence entirely, but the point is to minimize violence as much as possible.

Plants and vegetables also certainly have consciousness, but it is not as evolved as that of other living beings. Thus, the pain involved is minimal.

The degree of pain experienced by a living being depends on the development of the nervous system and since in plants and vegetables it is not significantly developed, the violence committed is the least, in contrast to the killing of other living entities.

In essence, it is true that all created beings, whether humans, animals or plants, are God's children and therefore the ideal situation would be to cause no violence; but we also need to subsist and thus we settle for the option where there is minimum violence.

Let us compare the atmosphere when fruits and vegetables are plucked with the gruesome atmosphere in a slaughterhouse. When animals are slaughtered, screaming and writhing in pain, their blood and flesh strewn all around, our own conscience and intelligence will make clear the vast difference between plucking vegetables and killing innocent animals.

What about the minimum violence or karma involved in consuming fruits and vegetables? Lord Krishna gives a solution in the Bhagavad Gita (3.13):

> yajna-shistashinah santo
> muchyante sarva-kilbishaih
> bhunjate te tv agham papa
> ye pachanty atma-karanat

'The devotees of the Lord are released from all kinds of sins because they eat food that is offered first for sacrifice. Others, who prepare food for personal sense enjoyment, verily eat only sin.'

Offer food to God before you eat it!

By doing so, whatever little karma is involved when we pluck and consume vegetables is nullified.

The Bhagavad Gita here is teaching us to go even beyond vegetarianism to be totally free from any karmic or sinful repercussions.

But those who don't offer food to God, as Lord Krishna says, will suffer sinful reactions due to whatever violence was involved, even if it is vegetarian food. So the best situation is to partake of vegetarian food produced with as little violence as possible and offer it first to the Lord with devotion so that it is not only vegetarian or karma-free but also pure and purifying.

Q. 7

What is the size of the soul?

The Shvetasvatara Upanishad (5.9) confirms:

> *balagra-shata-bhagasya*
> *shatadha kalpitasya ca*
> *bhago jivah sa vijneyah*
> *sa chanantyaya kalpate*

'When the upper point of a hair is divided into one
hundred parts and again each such part is further divided
into one hundred parts, that becomes the measurement
of the dimension of the soul.'

The same is stated in Srimad Bhagavatam:

> *keshagra-shata-bhagasya*
> *shatamsha-sadrishatmakaḥ*
> *jivah sukshma-svarupo 'yam*
> *sankhyatito hi chit-kanah*

25

'If we divide the tip of a hair into a hundred parts and
then take one of these parts and divide it again into
a hundred parts, that very fine division is the size of
but one of the numberless living entities. They are all
chit-kana or spiritual particles, not matter.'

Thus, the size of the soul is one ten-thousandth of the tip of
a hair.

However, the Bhagavad Gita (2.18) defines the soul as
'*aprameya*' or immeasurable. How do we understand this?

This means that the soul is spiritual and thus immeasurable
by material means. However, it does have dimensions and a
form and thus the scriptures also talk about its size.

The spiritual dimension is different from the material and
thus material measurements don't apply to the soul. Even if
we examine the heart with a microscope that can measure
one ten-thousandth of a tip of a hair, we will not be able to
detect the soul because material conceptions do not apply to
the soul. In that sense, the soul is immeasurable. But at the
same time the soul has a form and the form has dimensions
and that spiritual dimension has now become compressed in
one seed-like form inside a body.

How can we perceive its influence? Certainly not with
our blunt material and impure senses.

The Mundaka Upanishad (3.1.9) explains:

esho 'nur atma chetasa veditavyo
yasmin pranah panchadha savivesha

pranaish chittam sarvam otam prajanam
yasmin vishuddhe vibhavaty esha atma

'The soul is atomic in size and can be perceived by perfect intelligence. This atomic soul is floating in the five kinds of air (prāṇa, apāna, vyāna, samāna and udāna), is situated within the heart, and spreads its influence all over the body of the embodied living entities. When the soul is purified from the contamination of the five kinds of material air, its spiritual influence is exhibited.'

Q. 8

Is God formless or does He have a form?

'God' means a complete and a perfect personality with no room for any imperfection. If we say He has a form and no formless aspect, then we are limiting Him. If He is God, the all-powerful, why can't He have a formless aspect also? He could be anything that He wishes to. And saying He is formless and cannot have a form is also restricting Him. So to resolve the issue, we must refer to the scriptures, as the knowledge about God must come from them and not from social media, the opinion of the majority or our own limited perception.

Srimad Bhagavatam (1.2.12) answers:

vadanti tat tattva-vidas
tattvaṁ yaj jñānam advayam
brahmeti paramātmeti
bhagavān iti śabdyate

> 'Learned transcendentalists who know the Absolute
> Truth [God] call this non-dual substance Brahman,
> Paramātmā or Bhagavān.'

This means that God has a form, a formless aspect and something in between as well. That makes Him complete and perfect, not lacking in anything.

At the lowest level is the Brahman or the formless aspect, which people address as *Brahmajyoti* (the blue light). Higher than this is the localized aspect or *Paramatma* (the four-handed Vishnu form) situated in everyone's heart and upon which yogis meditate. And the highest aspect is Bhagwan or the personal aspect of the Lord where we know Him as a person full of six luxuries, namely, wealth, beauty, knowledge, strength, fame and renunciation.

Let us understand this with the help of an analogy of sunlight, the sun globe and the sun god (Surya Devata). The sunlight represents the Brahman aspect or the impersonal aspect of the sun. Study of the sunlight is not a complete study of the sun. It is the preliminary one. When we go closer, we find that there is a sun globe from where this light is coming, and that is like the Paramatma aspect. This entails slightly advanced study. When we enter the sun globe we see that there is a being, Surya Devata, who is controlling the affairs of the sun and that is like the Bhagwan aspect of the Lord. He, in this form, is making things happen for the sun globe to shine.

Just like sunlight is emitted by the sun and not the other way around, the formless aspect of God originated from the form and not otherwise.

To further clarify, let us refer to one of the most sacred scriptures, the Bhagavad Gita (12.1), where Arjuna asks Lord Krishna, 'Some worship your formless aspect and some engage in the devotional service of your personal form, which among the two are considered to be superior?'

Lord Krishna answers:

> *shri-bhagavan uvacha*
> *mayy aveshya mano ye mam*
> *nitya-yukta upasate*
> *shraddhaya parayopetas*
> *te me yukta-tama matah*

'The Supreme Personality of Godhead said: Those who fix their minds on My personal form and are always engaged in worshipping Me with great and transcendental faith are considered by Me to be the most perfect.'

Lord Brahma, the first created being in the universe, also clarifies in Brahma Samhita (5.40):

> *yasya prabha prabhavato jagad-anda-koti-*
> *kotisu ashesha-vasudhadi-vibhuti- bhinnam*
> *tad brahma nishkalam anantam ashesha-bhutam*
> *govindam adi-purusham tam aham bhajami*

'I worship Govinda, the primeval Lord, whose radiance is the source of the formless Brahman mentioned in

the Upanishads, being differentiated from the infinity
of glories of the mundane universe and appears as the
indivisible, infinite, limitless, truth.'

Thus, it is clear that the Supreme Lord has a form, worship
of the form is superior and that form is the source of the
formless aspect, just as a bulb is the cause behind the light
and not the other way around.

Now what about certain scriptures that talk about the
formless aspect and address God as *Nirakar* and *Nirgun*?

Well, we must understand that among scriptures also there
is a hierarchy of understanding, and each scripture caters to a
particular level of spiritual evolution. The Bhagavad Gita and
Srimad Bhagavatam are the foremost among the scriptures
and give complete knowledge about God. Other scriptures
touch upon a preliminary understanding with the goal of
guiding one towards the ultimate understanding. They bring
us to a certain level and then we are expected to advance and
not remain stuck with the preliminary knowledge.

When the scriptures say Nirakar or without form, this is
addressing those people who, due to a narrow understanding,
think that God also has a form like theirs and thus, try to
impose their own consciousness on Him and bring Him down
to a mundane or ordinary platform. Thus, to overcome such
ignorant thinking, the scriptures say, He is Nirakar Brahman
or Formless. This helps bring about a change in philosophical
outlook and helps develop reverence towards God.

So Nirakar means that the Lord does not have a mundane
form like ours, but He does have a spiritual form.

Again, quoting from the Brahma Samhita (5.1):

sac-cid-ānanda-vigrahaḥ
'The Lord has an eternal form, full of knowledge and
bliss.'

Vigrahah means 'form'.

Lord Brahma, who is the first created being within the
universe and thus knows more than everyone else, explains
that the Lord has a form, a divine form that is full of eternity,
knowledge and bliss (*satchidananda*).

When some scriptures use Nirgun, it does not mean that
the Lord has no qualities. It simply means that He has no
mundane qualities like us. There are three gunas (goodness,
passion and ignorance) that bind all of us. But God is beyond
them as He is supremely independent and thus cannot be
bound by anything. Hence, He is known as Nirgun.

Our father has a form. His father has a form and his father
had a form. So, if we go back to our roots and ancestors, we
see how everyone has had a form. When we say God has no
form, do we mean that the Supreme Lord does not have a
form? Is that not an absurd logic?

All the pastimes that the Lord has performed have been
performed in a form. All the instructions that He has ever
given, have been given in a form.

So if form is neither a reality nor relevant, why would
He emphasize it so much? Why would form be the primary
medium of His activities in this world?

And in conclusion, if God did not have a form, it would
be impossible to have any personal relationship with Him.

Q. 9

If God is everywhere, do we need to go to a temple?

Yes and no.

Water is a combination of hydrogen and oxygen. Hydrogen and oxygen are everywhere. When we feel thirsty, why don't we just open our mouth and suck in a little bit of hydrogen and oxygen to quench our thirst? The reason is that we need an accessible form of water. Similarly, although God is everywhere, we need an accessible form of God to access His grace, and the temple happens to be such a place. In a temple where the Lord is worshipped with a lot of love, care and attention, He will manifest His supreme mercy, beauty and blessings. So yes! We must go to such a temple on a regular basis to bathe ourselves in that divinity and be blessed.

However, if there is a temple where we find the standards are not maintained and the Lord's service is not up to the mark, then it will not manifest the Lord's grace, and thus we might not receive the divine touch an ideal temple can offer. So, we can certainly avoid such a place. But if we find a place that is charged with divine energy, then we must certainly make it a habit to visit it often and encourage others to do so as well.

We are all troubled by our turbulent minds and the temple is a hospital for the sick mind. The word for temple in Hindi is 'mandir', which comes from the word 'mann' meaning 'the mind'. Thus, a temple or mandir is a place where our 'mann' or 'mind' is cleansed.

Also, the temple serves as a battery charger. In our fast-paced lives, plagued as we are by so many issues, we get drained. Thus, we go to a temple to get recharged so we can execute our worldly duties with extra vigour.

The temple also serves as an educational institution that trains us in the spiritual culture so we can practise the same at home with our family members. As the famous saying goes, 'A family that prays together, stays together.'

And lastly, temples serve to remind us of the ultimate goal of human life, i.e., self-realization or God realization. Out of sight is out of mind. When we regularly come into contact with the divine atmosphere of the temple, we remain vigilant to the sacred principle that we must not only work, but simultaneously remember Him while we work. This will help us to be in this world, but not of this world, unaffected by the dualities of life. In time, our work will become worship.

Q. 10

How should one pray?

Prayers are powerful, so much so that they can alter a person's destiny. It is said, 'A prayer should be the steering wheel of our life, not a spare wheel.' It should be the key of the day and the lock of the night.

But what does it take to get our prayers answered? Let us understand the age-old secret.

Usually when we go in front of the Lord, we express our distress or desires. But this is not the ideal way to pray. Srimad Bhagavatam explains the sequence in which we should offer prayers to make sure that the Lord takes our prayers seriously and answers them in due course of time.

Following is the sequence in which we should offer our heartfelt prayers before expressing what we desire.

1. **Prayers of glorification:** The Supreme Lord is glorious, and the scriptures are full of His unlimited glories. When we go in front of any exalted person, we must say something in His praise. Similarly, when we are in

front of the Lord, we should first glorify Him for his name, fame, beauty, qualities, pastimes and His causeless compassion.

The scriptures have many such beautiful prayers, and we can memorize them. If we cannot, we can glorify Him in our own words because ultimately it is the intention to glorify that matters.

Example of a prayer of glorification:

> *namah pankaja-nabhaya namah pankaja-maline*
> *namah pankaja-netraya namas te pankajanghraye*

'My respectful obeisance is unto You, O Lord, whose abdomen is marked with a depression like a lotus flower, who is always decorated with garlands of lotus flowers, whose glance is as cool as the lotus and whose feet are engraved with lotuses.'

2. **Prayers of gratitude:** Secondly, we should offer our immense gratitude to the Lord and thank Him for whatever he has blessed us with. If we look around, we will see that we have so many blessings starting with this human body, a nice family, facilities, food, shelter, friends and so on.

Expressing gratitude for anything we receive is a sign of culture. If someone gives us a glass of water, we say 'thank you'. Similarly, God has given us so much to sustain our life. Thus, it is only appropriate that we acknowledge it and thank Him from time to time.

Example of a prayer of gratitude:

pratijna tava govinda na me bhaktah pranashyati
iti samsmritya samsmritya pranan sandharayamy aham

'O Govinda, Your promise is that Your devotee will
never perish. By remembering this over and over again, I
am able to retain my life.

3. **Prayers for forgiveness:** To err is human. Knowingly or
unknowingly, we end up committing so many mistakes.
With our thoughts, words and actions, we end up hurting
and exploiting other living beings, sometimes even
without having such intentions. We should therefore seek
forgiveness from the Lord for all the wrongs that we have
done and thus humble ourselves before Him. To forgive
is divine. And humility is one quality that softens His
heart like nothing else. No matter what we have done,
if we are humble, and seek forgiveness, He will certainly
forgive as He is extremely kind. But our repentance and
seeking mercy should be based on resolving not to repeat
the mistake.

An example of a prayer for forgiveness:

aparadha sahasrani
kriyante 'har nisham maya
daso 'ham iti mam matva
kshamasva madhusudana

'Thousands of offenses are performed by me day and
night, but thinking of me as Your servant, kindly forgive
those, O Madhusudana!'

And lastly:

4. **Express your desire:** Now that we have glorified the
    Lord, acknowledged His blessings by thanking Him and
    even accepted our wrongs, we can express what we desire.
    We all know that when a person is in a happy mood, the
    chances of them giving what another wants are greater.
    By offering the first three types of prayers, we please the
    Lord and thus He is more than happy to pay attention
    to our prayers and grant them as and when He sees fit.
    His timing and his method of reciprocating with what
    we desire are always perfect. But most importantly, even
    after expressing our desire, we should end all prayers with
    one line and that is, 'My dear Lord! Now do whatever
    You think is best for me or my family.' And rest assured
    that He will certainly do the best since only He knows
    what is best. He has promised in the Srimad Bhagavatam,
    'Anyone who develops love for me, I must fulfil all his
    desires.' So instead of asking from the Lord straight away,
    we should do something to please Him and when He is
    pleased with us, He will be kind enough to grant our
    wishes.

Q. 11

Why don't we remember our past lives?

Firstly, it is our tendency to forget; can we remember what we were doing at this very moment one year ago, one month ago or even one week ago? Unlikely. Similarly, to remember our past lives is very difficult, if not impossible. But, just because we can't remember a past event doesn't prove the non-occurrence of that event.

Also, it is our innate psychological defence mechanism to forget painful incidents; in this very life, we get over traumas by forgetting them with the passage of time. Between our present and past lives lies the trauma of death. Suppose we had died in a car accident and could remember it; we would likely be paranoid of cars throughout our lives. To save us from such psychological malfunctioning, nature arranges to erase our past-life memories.

Souls come into this world to enjoy it and to do this, it is necessary to forget. We do not have any account of how many lives we have spent in this world or how many bad experiences we have gone through in those lives, how much

39

we have suffered or caused others to suffer. If we were to remember just one wrong thing that we had done or that had happened to us, it would become difficult to eat or sleep or enjoy anything. What if we started remembering everything? By remembering our mistakes, we keep living in the past, and this could lead to depression. It will be very difficult for us to move on and enjoy or create a new life.

The Lord's creation is complete as the Ishopanishad (Invocation) says:

om purnam adah purnam idam purnat purnam udacyate
purnasya purnam adaya purnam evavasisyate

'The Personality of Godhead is perfect and complete, and because He is completely perfect, all emanations from Him, such as this phenomenal world, are perfectly equipped as complete wholes. Whatever is produced of the Complete Whole is also complete in itself. Because He is the Complete Whole, even though so many complete units emanate from Him, He remains the complete balance.'

There is no loophole within the Lord's creation. So, if He has introduced an error or a hurdle, there must be a reason.

Imagine the chaos if everyone started remembering their past lives and recognizing that the next-door neighbour was the one who killed them or that the person in the next building was the one they were married to. Would anyone's life be normal? It would truly drive us insane.

For new beginnings, forgetfulness of the past is necessary.

There have been many cases of reincarnation where children have started remembering their past lives. This may sound exciting, but if we ask those children about the experience, they will say it is a miserable one because they have to live a double life. They remember a past they can't go back to, and they live a present life they cannot relate to. So let us trust the system made by the Lord and carry on with our lives, remembering that whatever situation the Lord has put us in is the best for our growth.

Q. 12

Who is the supreme: Lord Vishnu or Lord Krishna?

Essentially, they are the same person in two different roles. Lord Vishnu is God at office and Lord Krishna is God at home. But still one of Them is the origin of the other.

Many people believe that Lord Vishnu is the source of all the incarnations including Lord Krishna. But, as we have mentioned before, our information on such matters must be authoritative and authentic, and it is so only when it comes from the scriptures and not from the internet or social media platforms.

The scriptures describe Lord Krishna to be the source of all incarnations.

So where does Lord Vishnu fit in the picture?

Following is the hierarchy as given in the great scripture Chaitanya Charitamrita(CC);

Krishna is the origin Who then expands into Balaram.

vaibhava-prakasha krishnera—shri-balarama
(CCMadhya Lila 20.174)

'The first manifestation of the vaibhava feature of Kṛṣṇa
is Śrī Balarāmajī.'

Lord Balaram then expands into four other forms known
as the first quadruple expansion: Vasudev I, Sankarshan 1,
Pradyumna 1 and Aniruddha I.

prabhava-vilasa—vasudeva, sankarshana
pradyumna, aniruddha,—mukhya chari-jana
(CC Madhya 20.186)

'The chief quadruple expansions are named Vaudeva,
Sankarshana, Pradyumna and Aniruddha. These are
called prabhava-vilasa.'

Lord Krishna again expands into two features:

1) Narayan—He becomes the cause of the manifestations
   of all the countless Lord Vishnu forms in Vaikuntha
   (Spiritual Sky)
2) Second Quadruple expansion (Expansions of the first
   quadruple expansions)—Vaudeva II, Sankarshana II,
   Pradyumna II and Aniruddha II

punah krishna chatur-vyuha laian purva-rupe
paravyoma-madhye vaise narayana-rupe
(CC Madhya 20.192)

'Lord Kṛṣṇa again expands, and within the paravyoma,
the spiritual sky, He is situated in fullness as the four-
handed Narayaṇa, accompanied by expansions of the
original quadruple form.'

tanha haite punaḥ chatur-vyuha-parakasha
avarana-rupe chari-dike yanra vasa
(CC Madhya 20.193)

'Thus the original quadruple forms again manifest
Themselves in a second set of quadruple expansions-
Vaudeva II, Sankarshana II, Pradyumna II and
Aniruddha II.'

From Lord Sankarshan II come two personalities: Sadashiv
(the original Shiva) and Lord Mahavishnu.

viṣṇos tu trīṇi rūpāṇi
puruṣākhyāny atho viduḥ
ekaṁ tu mahataḥ sraṣṭṛ
dvitīyaṁ tv aṇḍa-saṁsthitam
tṛtīyaṁ sarva-bhūta-sthaṁ
tāni jñātvā vimucyate
(CC Madhya 20.251)

'Viṣṇu has three forms called puruṣas. The first, Mahā-
Viṣṇu, is the creator of the total material energy [mahat],
the second is Garbhodaśāyī, who is situated within each
universe, and the third is Kṣīrodaśāyī, who lives in the

> heart of every living being. He who knows these three
> becomes liberated from the clutches of māyā.'

Lord Mahavishnu then takes charge of creating countless universes from His body and expands Himself to enter each of the universes where He lies down at the bottom of the universe in an ocean called Garbodhak.

From the naval of this second Lord Vishnu, called Garbhodakshayi Vishnu, emerges a lotus upon which Lord Brahma is born, who, as the secondary creator, further creates the living entities in the universe.

Garbhodakshayi Vishnu then expands Himself into another form of Lord Vishnu known as Kshirodakshayi Vishnu, the one who resides in the ocean of milk. It is He who is responsible for the maintenance of the universe He is residing in.

Whenever there is a need, Kshirodakshayi Vishnu incarnates into the universes to uphold dharma.

All this information tells us that there are countless and not just one Lord Vishnu, just as there are countless universes. In fact, there are two forms of Lord Vishnu in each Universe. And the particular Lord Vishnu form whom everyone knows to be the maintainer comes much later in the picture, i.e., Kshirodakshayi Vishnu. Further, Lord Krishna, being the supreme source of all avatars, has sixty-four primary qualities and Lord Vishnu, being an expansion has sixty.

The Shata-nama-stotra says:

> *vishnor ekaikam namapi sarva-vedadhikam matam*
> *tadrik-nama sahasrena rama-nama-samam smritam*

'Chanting one name of Vishnu gives more benefit
thanstudying all the Vedas, and one name of Rama is
equal to athousand names (sahasra-nama) of Vishnu.'

Again, it is stated in the Brahmanda Purana:

sahasra-namnam punyanam trir avrittya tu yat phalam
ekavrittya tu krishnasya namaikam tat prayacchati

'If one utters shri-krishna-nama once, one obtains the
sameresult that comes from chanting the pure visnu-
sahasranamathree times.'

The purport is that a thousand names of Lord Vishnu equals
one name of Lord Rama, and three thousand names of Lord
Vishnu—or three names of Lord Rama—equals one name of
Lord Krishna. Chanting Lord Krishna's name once gives the
same result as chanting Lord Rama's name three times.

This result is due to Lord Krishna being the source of all
avatars.

The Srimad Bhagavatam contains a list of various avatars
after which Lord Krishna is again referred to as 'svayam bhagavan',
which means He is the source of all other forms of Bhagwan
such as Vishnu, Varaha, Narasihma, Rama and Vamana.

ete camsha-kalah pumsah
krishnas tu bhagavan svayam
indrari-vyakulam lokam
mridayanti yuge yuge

'All of the above-mentioned incarnations are either
plenary portions or portions of the plenary portions of
the Lord, but Lord Śrī Kṛṣṇa is the original Personality
of Godhead. All of them appear on planets whenever
there is a disturbance created by the atheists. The Lord
incarnates to protect the theists.'

In the Brahma Samhita (5.1), Lord Brahma mentions:

ishvarah paramah krishnah
sac-cid-ananda-vigrahaha
anadir adir govindaha
sarva-karana-karanam

'Krishna who is known as Govinda is the Supreme
Godhead. He has an eternal blissful spiritual body. He
is the origin of all. He has no other origin, and He is the
prime cause of all causes.'

If this is so clearly mentioned in the scriptures, why is there
confusion about the position of Lord Vishnu and Lord
Krishna?

Well, the reason is quite simple.

Lord Vishnu is in charge of the maintenance of the
universe; He is hands-on in this world and every now and
then He incarnates.

It is just like in a factory, the workers receive orders and
payment from their manager. To them, he is their leader, the
person in charge of it all. However, one fine day, the owner

of the factory decides to visit the factory. When the workers see that person next to the manager, they don't recognize him because they haven't seen him before.

Similarly, although it is Lord Vishnu who is incarnating into this world to sustain it, once in a while, Lord Krishna personally comes down from the supreme spiritual abode of Golok Vrindavan along with all His associates. And when He comes down, He comes through Lord Vishnu who also makes the announcement for the same.

When the world was overburdened five thousand years ago due to demoniac forces, mother earth and the demigods including Lord Brahma and Lord Shiva went to the shore of the ocean of milk (Kshirsagar) to pray to Kshirodakshayi Vishnu. After they offered their prayers for the Lord's mercy, Lord Brahma received a message from Him, which He related to everyone present as follows:

vasudeva-grihe sakshad
bhagavan purushah parah
janishyate tat-priyartham
sambhavantu sura-striyah

[Srimad Bhagavatam 10.1.23]

'The Supreme Personality of Godhead, Śrī Kṛṣṇa, who has full potency, will personally appear as the son of Vasudeva. Therefore, all the wives of the demigods should also appear in order serve Him.'

Thus, since Lord Krishna is seen only once in a while and Lord Vishnu is visible and active most of the time, people have the misconception that Lord Vishnu is the source of Lord Krishna, but the truth is, it is the other way around.

Q. 13

Why did Lord Krishna have 16,108 wives?

Lord Krishna has stated in the Bhagavad Gita, 'As all surrender unto me, I reward them accordingly.'

Being God, it is His duty to reciprocate with everyone as per their desire and to give shelter to whoever asks for it.

Many ages ago, 16,100 princesses were abducted by the demon Narakasur. While in captivity, the princesses constantly prayed to the Lord to save them as there was no one else who could rescue them. The omniscient Lord Krishna, who was residing in Dwarka at the time, heard their prayers. He killed this demon and rescued the princesses.

After being saved, the princesses prayed to Lord Krishna to accept them, as society, being bound by certain traditions, would not accept them after they had been with a demon for such a long time.

Lord Krishna, who is infinitely merciful, accepted their proposal and hence married all of them.

His other eight principal queens, namely, Rukmini, Satyabhama, Jambavati, Kalindi, Nagnajiti, Bhadra, Mitravinda and Laxmana, were also not approached by Lord Krishna for marriage. Each one of these queens prayed fervently to marry Lord Krishna, and He, being the Supreme Lord, was duty-bound to reciprocate.

Thus, Lord Krishna ended up marrying 16,108 queens. But remember, He married them because they wanted to marry Him. He is known as *Atmaram*, one who is self-satisfied, and thus does not need any outside sources to feel satisfied.

When we see Him engaging in such affairs, we must understand that there is a higher principle at work, that is of the Supreme Lord simply performing his most exalted pastime of pleasing His dear devotees. He is *bhava-grahi*—he accepts our intentions and responds accordingly.

Q. 14

Why did Lord Krishna engage in the Raas Lila, dancing with the gopis in the middle of the night?

The same scriptures that talk about Lord Krishna's Raas Lila also talk about Him being the Supreme Lord, capable of accomplishing impossible tasks. A devotee can enter into any relationship with Him, and He is always there to reciprocate proportionately.

Each devotee worships the Lord in a unique mood. Some devotees wish to serve Him as their master and some wish to enter into a relationship with Him as a friend, as did Subal, Sridama, Arjuna and others. Some wish to serve Him as parents like Yashoda-Nanda and Devaki-Vasudev, whereas some like the gopis desire to see Him as their beloved. In all cases, Lord Krishna is simply reciprocating with the desires of His dear devotees. So essentially, there is no difference between Lord Krishna's dealing with the peacocks and parrots of Vrindavan, His receiving service from His servants like Raktak, Him being cared for by Yashoda and

Nanda, or Him dancing (Raas Lila) in great joy with the gopis of Vrindavan. All are on the same platform because in all of these, there is nothing but His reciprocation with the devotees as they desire.

Instead of criticizing Him for His Raas Lila, we should feel happy that our kind Lord is ready to go to any extent to satisfy His devotees' desires, and if we also desire a particular type of reciprocation from Him, we shall receive the same. So, the Raas Lila of the Lord should fill us with hope rather than remorse.

In addition, the gopis of the Raas Lila were not ordinary girls. They were Lord Krishna's own energies who, for the sake of pastimes or lilas, had descended with Him from the spiritual world. Thus, there is no harm if Krishna He is dancing with His own shaktis or energies.

Also, if this pastime is immoral as many think, why would it find a place in such a great scripture as Srimad Bhagavatam, in which the chapters describing the Raas Lila are considered to be the best?

If the Raas Lila were immoral, why would great renunciants such as Sukdev Goswami and many others even talk about and glorify it?

The reality is that this pastime or any pastime of Krishna is enacted on a spiritual platform, and from a mundane platform, it is very difficult to comprehend. As Krishna confirms in the Bhagavad Gita (4.9):

janma karma cha me divyam
evam yo vetti tattvatah

tyaktva deham punar janma
naiti mam eti so 'rjuna

'One who knows the divine nature of My appearance
and activities does not, upon leaving the body, take his
birth again in this material world, but attains My eternal
abode, O Arjuna.'

Anyone who can understand the truth behind Lord Krishna's
activities achieves liberation. This goes to show that this
understanding is not easy. We have to dive deeper as explained
above.

If He was too eager for the Raas Lila, why would He
disappear from it as soon as the gopis developed subtle
spiritual pride? He clearly indicated that he was not attached
to it and was there simply because the gopis prayed for it.

If Lord Krishna was at fault for indulging in the Raas
Lila, why would great beings such as Lord Shiva, Narada and
Goddess Laxmi participate in it? When we see such great
beings participating in an event, we can only conclude that
the event must be special.

When people find fault with Lord Krishna and consider
Him to be immoral on account of His Raas Lila, we must
understand that the same scriptures that describe the Raas
Lila also talk about Him as God who is faultless, as the lifter
of the gigantic Govardhan Lila, as the God dancing on the
thousand-hooded serpent Kaliya or killing ferocious demons
when He was just three days old, all of which are strong
evidence of His divinity. But some people, to demean the
Lord and justify His atheism, conveniently select a particular

episode and ignore others from the same scripture. They say, 'Oh, it is false. How could He lift a mountain?' Just because something is impossible for us does not mean it is impossible for everyone else, and certainly not for the Supreme Lord. If we accept one part of the scripture, we have to accept the other parts too. As one great saint said, 'You either be hot or be cold. If you are lukewarm, I spit you out.' So either we believe everything from the scriptures or we do not believe at all.

When we see the Lord engaging in an activity that is difficult to make sense of, rather than accusing Him and implicating ourselves in the karmic cycle, we should be humble, thinking, 'Oh! I am so ignorant that I cannot understand why the Lord is doing this!' As a second step, we should approach a dedicated devotee of the Lord for an explanation as only His devotees can understand and explain the truth about Him.

Srimad Bhagavatam (7.15.28) explains:

> *yasya deve para bhaktir*
> *yatha deve tatha gurau*
> *tasyaite kathita hy arthah*
> *prakashante mahatmanah*

'Only unto those great souls who have implicit faith in both the Lord and the spiritual master are all the imports of the Vedic knowledge automatically revealed.'

In essence, the Raas Lila is a purely spiritual, loving reciprocation between the Lord and His dear devotees enacted beyond the platform of our limited, ordinary understanding.

Q. 15

In the Ramayana, why did Lord Rama kill Vali from behind a tree?

Lord Rama's killing of Vali is elaborately discussed in Valmiki's Ramayana and has been analysed by many great spiritual teachers.

Due to a misunderstanding between Vali and Sugriva, the two inseparable brothers, the older and stronger Vali had driven Sugriva from their kingdom and was constantly seeking to eliminate him forever. Sugriva had to live in fear until Lord Rama, who was sent into exile, arrived and promised to help Sugriva restore peace in his life, which could only happen when Vali was killed as all efforts for a reconciliation had failed. As per the Lord's arrangement, Sugriva challenged Vali to a combat, but he was defeated and barely managed to escape with his life. On the urging of the Lord, Sugriva challenged his brother again. When the fight was in progress, Lord Rama hid behind a tree and shot an arrow that struck Vali, who immediately collapsed to the ground. He was furious as he had been shot at in a cowardly manner, and he questioned Lord Rama about the religious principles guiding the codes of battle.

This one act does seem to be a stain on the otherwise spotless and virtuous character of Lord Rama, but the Ramayana offers a simple explanation behind the Lord's act.

After being hit, Vali falls to the ground in pain and looks around. He sees Lord Rama approaching him with a smile on His face. In a fit of rage and agony Vali says, 'I thought you were a virtuous person. How could you have done something so vicious? I think it is because of your association with this terrible person Sugriva that you have also become spoiled.'

Lord Rama smiles and He says, 'O Vali, it seems that with the deterioration of the body even the intelligence deteriorates. You are accusing me of immorality without understanding the intricacies of dharma.' Lord Rama further says, 'I am the servant of Bharata who is the ruler of the world. So as a member of the royal order and a servant of the king, it is my duty to protect the virtuous and to punish the unrighteous or the vicious. You, O monkey, have for no reason whatsoever grievously wronged your faithful younger brother Sugriva. Although there was no fault of his, you attacked, insulted, exiled and threatened to take his very life. If that was not enough, you even took up his wife as your wife. And because of all this, you are an aggressor.'

The Vedic scriptures describe six types of aggressors, and even if they are killed by those who are meant to be upholders of the law, there is no sin incurred. They are: one who kidnaps another's wife, administers poison, attacks with deadly weapons, sets fire to the house, steals property or steals wealth. When a policeman arrests a criminal, he is not punished by the law for doing so. The kshatriyas are like the policeman and the aggressors are like the criminals. Since Vali grievously wronged his brother for no good reason, it was Lord Rama's duty to kill him and to give justice to Sugriva. Thus, Vali was killed and the means were justified.

And then the Lord says, 'You are a monkey, and as a hunter, I can kill an animal without necessarily confronting it, while being in a tree or being concealed in the bushes. The kshatriya codes allow one to do that. That is why I have killed you and I have done nothing wrong.'

Finally, Lord Rama says, 'O Vali, if you still feel that I have wronged you, then I can give you back your life right now.'

But upon hearing what Lord Rama had said, Vali accepted his sins and hung his head in shame. He even admitted that he himself had often felt that he had wronged Sugriva, but his ego had not allowed him to apologize. He expressed his happiness that he was leaving his body in the Lord's presence. He left, but not before reconciling with Sugriva and expressing his regret over what he had done.

Vali's source of power had been a special necklace. As long as he was wearing it, he could not die. That was how he was able to stay alive even after being pierced by Lord Rama's arrow, and that was how he could talk with him for so long. Vali took that necklace and gave it not to his own son, but to Sugriva. It would have been natural for him to give it to his son; nobody would have blamed him for doing so because the necklace would have made his son invincible. But Vali was so transformed by Lord Rama's answer that he realized he had wronged Sugriva and to seek forgiveness, he gave his brother the necklace. Before giving it, he told Angada, his son, 'Don't bear any animosity towards Sugriva or Lord Rama because they have not killed me. It is my own bad deeds that have caused my death. Please serve Sugriva as you have served me and please serve Lord Rama as the Supreme Lord.'

Another question still remains. Why did Lord Rama have to kill Vali stealthily and not directly in battle?

Vali had earlier performed tapasya and in return had received blessings from the celestial gods. He had wanted immortality, but the gods could not grant it to him as they themselves were not immortal. So he asked for immortality in an indirect way by asking for half of his opponents' powers whenever they fought him. Through this clever trick, Vali ensured his victory always. Lord Rama is the Supreme Lord, and He could still have killed Vali anyway, but he honoured the benedictions of the devatas which stated that anyone who came in front of Vali would lose half of his powers to Vali and thus Vali could never be defeated. The Lord was playing the part of a human being and thus He acted as if He too would have been affected by this benediction.

Q. 16

What happens after death?

Death is a reality that no one wants to talk about, but also something that no one can avoid. Some people believe that life is over after death, and this is the only life we have. However, the scriptures, which are the word of God and our guidebooks, say differently.

In fact, this is one of the first topics Lord Krishna discusses in the Bhagavad Gita (2.13):

dehino 'smin yatha dehe kaumaram yauvanam jara
tatha dehantara-praptir dhiras tatra na muhyati

'As the embodied soul continuously passes, in this body,
from boyhood to youth to old age, the soul similarly
passes into another body at death. An intelligent person
is not bewildered by such a change.'

He also says in the Bhagavad Gita (2.27):

jatasya hi dhruvo mrityur
dhruvam janma mritasya cha
tasmad apariharye 'rthe
na tvam shocitum arhasi

'One who has taken his birth is sure to die, and after death, one is sure to take birth again. Therefore, in the unavoidable discharge of your duty, you should not lament.'

The body goes through a change at every moment, and death is the final change after which the soul enters another body. But the type of body the soul gets will depend on one's actions in this life.

According to Padma Puran, there are 8.4 million types of bodies:

jalaja nava lakshani, sthavara laksha-vimshati, krimayo
rudra-sankhyakah, pakshinam dasha-lakshanam, trinshal-
lakshani pashavah, chatur lakshani manavah

Jalaja (water-based) – 0.9 million
Sthaavara (immobile, such as plants and trees) –
2.0 million
Krimaayo (reptiles) – 1.1 million
Pakshinaam (birds) – 1.0 million
Paashavah (terrestrial animals) – 3.0 million
Maanavah (human-like animals, including the human
species) – 0.4 million

Depending on the kind of activities we engage in, we develop a particular type of consciousness, based on which we get our next body. Once born as a human being does not necessarily mean we will always be born as a human being.

Just as we have a system of justice, reward and punishment in this world, the same system is present on a universal level. When we engage in good karma, enjoyment in the heavenly planets and a resultant good birth is the reward. When we engage in bad karma, knowingly or unknowingly, suffering in the hellish planets and a degraded birth (human or non-human) thereafter in this world is the punishment.

And for someone who engages in the devotional service of Lord Krishna, the spiritual world, where there is no suffering, where life is eternal with no old age, disease or death, is the reward.

How well or badly we lived in our previous life will decide where we begin. Due to this reason, everyone has a different starting point in life. Some are born rich and some are born poor, some are born healthy and some are born with diseases, some are born beautiful and some are not-so-beautiful and so on.

Thus, there is life after death, which is why the scriptures urge us to live responsibly and become mindful of our words and actions. And the righteousness of our words and actions should not be decided by social media, the majority or popular opinion, but by the scriptures, as ultimately everything will be judged based on what they say is right or wrong.

Q. 17

Why do bad things happen to good people?

The simple answer is our past karma. Let us understand this with an analogy.

In villages, people use huge granaries to store their grains. The specialty of these granaries is that we pour grains into them from the top, but when we need to take some out, we do so through a hole at the bottom, which is closed with a cover.

Suppose we had put 'D' quality grains into the granary a week ago, 'C' quality grains four days ago, 'B' quality grains two days ago and 'A' quality grains three hours ago. And suddenly, we want our 'A' quality grains, which we know we recently put into the granary. So, we open the cover at the bottom in excitement and lo and behold! What comes out? The 'D' quality grains. As we continue to take the grains out, we get to the 'C' quality grains, and we get frustrated because we cannot understand why we are not getting our 'A' quality grains, which we put into the granary just a few hours ago.

This is how the law of karma also works. Despite us being the best versions of ourselves, living a pious life and not harming anyone, we sometimes have to go through traumas, and we cannot figure out the cause, which is frustrating as we have been so good our whole life. And someone who is a cheater, who lives a life of sin, is living a prosperous life. Why?

We need to understand that just as in a granary, where the grains that were poured first will come out first, and only when the previous stock is exhausted will the recently added grains come out, so also in this life, our previous stock of karma will play out first. And once that stock is over, the results of our present activities will manifest.

So just because we are not experiencing happiness despite being honest in this life, we should not get disappointed and give up.

And just because someone is living a great life despite being on the wrong side, we should not be discouraged. They are only enjoying the results of their previous good karma, but as soon as that stock runs out, their life will become topsy-turvy.

Every act performed is like sowing a seed. What we sow is what we shall reap. But the seeds do not fructify as soon as they are sown.

Q. 18

How can we control our jealousy and ego?

By understanding that our abilities and the abilities of others come from God and thus, they belong to Him.

In the Bhagavad Gita (10.42), Lord Krishna says:

yad yad vibhutimat sattvam shrimad urjitam eva va
tat tad evavagachchha tvam mama tejo 'nsha-sambhavam

'Whatever you see as beautiful, glorious, or powerful,
know it to spring from but a spark of My splendour.'

Whatever gifts we have, such as good looks, speech, memory, wealth and so on, are gifts from Lord Krishna. If we remember this, we will always remember to be humble and have no ego. We must feel grateful to God for whatever gifts He has given us, and we must ideally use them to connect ourselves back to Him. This attitude will bring us greater happiness than the happiness that we might otherwise get by bragging about our abilities and trying to attract respect and praise from others.

When we see good qualities in others, we must remember the same principle. This is God's grace upon them and how wonderfully our dear Lord is manifesting through them. So instead of becoming jealous, we can use this situation to remember the Lord. And the more we remember Him, the more our hearts will become purified of vices such as ego and envy, and we can become positively enlivened and joyful. We can think: this person has this quality and because of this, so many people are attracted to them. But this quality is just a spark of the quality that Lord Krishna has. So, if this person with a spark can attract so many people, how much more attractive would Lord Krishna be?

If we see someone who has more than us, we can also think that they deserve it. The person must have performed very good karma in their previous life or worked hard in this one. So they deserve the blessings they have at present. This can be inspiring because it reveals that hard work pays off. If we work on ourselves, we can reap the same rewards as well.

We can also think that the other person needs more than us to carry on in life. After all, everyone has a story they might never tell.

Q. 19

Can I be spiritual without being religious?

Spirituality, as the word indicates, is that which is connected with the spirit, the soul and God, which are all realities existing on the spiritual platform.

Religion refers to those processes and actions that help one to come to the spiritual platform.

Many people in modern times think of spirituality as anything that makes them feel good—'I went to a mountainside resort, it was a very spiritual place.' Why? 'Because it made me feel good.' That is not spiritual. The Bhagavad Gita explains that spiritual knowledge begins with understanding that we are not the body, but the soul. So spirituality is the whole realm connected with the spirit—soul, God, their spiritual relationship, and how that relationship can be revived.

Religion, on the other hand, refers to those activities that help one connect with the higher spiritual reality. For example, the concept of praying, chanting God's names, worshipping or meditating on His form, associating with devotees on the same path and so on. These activities could be expressed differently in different religions. The Hindus may pray by folding their hands, the Muslims may pray by raising their hands, the Christians may pray by moving their hands across their face and chest during mass.

Just as science has two aspects—theory and experiment—spirituality also has two aspects—philosophy and religion. Philosophy tells us we are not the body, but the soul. And the soul can experience its highest happiness in relationship with God in divine love. Religion gives us the practical means and methods by which we can either confirm or disconfirm this particular point of philosophy.

Nowadays it is fashionable to say, 'I am spiritual but I am not religious.' While this may appear non-sectarian and broad-minded, if one does not have some method by which to gain spiritual realization, then the statement is equivalent to saying that I am scientific, but I am not experimental. Without experiment, science remains in the realm of unverified speculations. Similarly, spirituality without some form of religious expression or activities remains just theoretical, hypothetical philosophy.

Q. 20

Why did Lord Krishna not marry Radharani?

Before we answer this question, we need to understand who Radharani (also known as Radha) is.

Most people consider Radharani to be an ordinary cowherd girl and try to apply a mundane understanding to Her personality.

However, Radharani is none other than the 'adi-shakti' or original energy of Lord Krishna. In fact, She is not different from Him. In other words, She is God in the female form. Whenever Lord Krishna comes to this world, She accompanies him to engage in beautiful, loving pastimes along with the other gopis who are Her incarnations.

Chaitanya Charitamrita (1.5) describes:

radha krishna-pranaya-vikritir hladini shaktir asmad
ekatmanav api bhuvi pura deha-bhedam gatau tau

'The loving affairs of Shri Radha and Krishna are
transcendental manifestations of the Lord's internal

> pleasure-giving potency. Although Radha and Krishna
> are one in Their identity, previously They separated
> Themselves.'

Despite being the Supreme Lord, Lord Krishna engages in enchanting pastimes in Vrindavan as a fun-loving, carefree, youthful cowherd boy and Radharani becomes a cowherd girl.

However, in Dwarka, Lord Krishna has a more sober role to play as a king, and a king needs a queen. But not just anyone can become His queen. So, the Puranas describe in detail how the gopis of Vrindavan appeared as queens in Dwarka to marry Him. Radharani appeared as Satyabhama and Chandravali gopi became Rukmini in Dwarka.

Also, even if we consider the Vrindavan affairs, the Brahma Vaivarta Purana (Chapter 15) clearly describes the marriage ceremony of Radha and Lord Krishna that took place in Bhandirvan forest under a banyan tree, which still stands in Vrindavan. The marriage ceremony was performed by Lord Brahma as the priest, but it was not a public affair. Only a few of the closest gopis were blessed with this spectacle.

But despite these references, if someone does not believe these scriptural references, then we must understand that the rules of the material realm cannot be applied to the spiritual realm. Even within this material world, different countries can have different rules and within a country, every state can have separate rules. Similarly, the spiritual realm is different and most exalted. Radharani is eternally related to Lord Krishna as His shakti/potency and is never separate from

Him. Hence, there is no need for any formalization of this relationship.

When Radha-Krishna come to this world, They act as human beings but we should not think They are humans and certainly we should not try to bind Them with the insignificant ropes of our limited logic.

This is also why what They do is called lila or pastime and what we do is called karma.

Q. 21

Do all paths lead to the same goal?

A common notion about the Bhagavad Gita and about Vedic traditions in general is that 'all paths lead to the same goal'. Although this might sound like a liberal or broad-minded statement, it has no logical basis.

If we sit on a flight to Kolkata, we will not reach Delhi. If all paths lead to the same goal, why do we need to choose a particular flight to a specific destination? In our daily life also, we are choosy about what we buy and where we buy it from, we send our children to a particular school or we choose a particular holiday destination. So, if every path could lead to the same destination, why do we need so much planning? Surprisingly, we do not make such a statement when it comes to our personal life, but when it comes to spiritual life, something we do not have much idea about, we believe we can say anything. Whatever we say must have an authentic source. When it comes to spirituality or anything related to it, scriptures must be the basis.

In the Bhagavad Gita (9.25), Lord Krishna clearly says:

yanti deva-vrata devan
pitrn yanti pitr-vratah
bhutani yanti bhutejya
yanti mad-yajino 'pi mam

'Those who worship the demigods will take birth among the demigods; those who worship the ancestors go to the ancestors; those who worship ghosts and spirits will take birth among such beings; and those who worship Me will live with Me.'

Here Lord Krishna says, 'Whatever people worship is the situation they will get'. Those who worship Lord Krishna will attain Him. This verse clearly indicates that different paths lead to different ends.

Furthermore, He says in 7.23:

antavat tu phalam tesam
tad bhavaty alpa-medhasam
devan deva-yajo yanti
mad-bhakta yanti mam api

'Men of small intelligence worship the demigods, and their fruits are limited and temporary. Those who worship the demigods go to the planets of the demigods, but My devotees ultimately reach My supreme planet.'

This verse clearly states that different types of worship yield different results. If someone worships the demigods, the results are different from those attained if someone worships Him. Even though externally the worship looks the same, the rewards one gets will depend on the person one is serving. For example, someone who cooks in a roadside restaurant and someone who cooks in the home of the wealthiest man in the world are performing the same activity, but the rewards of each will be entirely different.

Yes, there are different paths and modes of worship mentioned in the scriptures, but since not everyone is spiritually evolved to the highest level, these different paths facilitate their gradual elevation towards the ultimate goal of engaging in the devotional service of the Lord (Bhakti Yoga). There is no harm in following them as long as we remember the goal and keep progressing.

But if a person thinks that being stuck at on a particular path without advancing itself is perfection, then that person gets a different result from the ones who are engaged in the highest path of Bhakti Yoga.

Normally, people on the path of good karma will achieve prosperity in this world or attain the heavenly planets and demigods (since good karmas are under their jurisdiction) in the next world. The path of jnana, cultivating knowledge, mind control, sense control etc, will lead to liberation and merger with Brahman, the formless aspect of God. The path of Ashtang Yoga/mystic or Dhyan Yoga will help one attain supernatural powers initially and then achieve spiritual realization. If a yogi thinks that he will merge with the Parmatma, then he goes to *brahmajyoti* or the blue effulgence, referring to the formless aspect of God also known as Brahman. If he understands that he is the servant of Parmatma or 'supersoul', then he goes to Vaikuntha. And of course, if someone is a devotee, then he goes directly to the spiritual world to be an eternal associate of Lord Krishna.

So, do all paths lead to the same goal? Yes, if one knows that goal well. If karmis, yogis and jyanis all know that their ultimate goal is Lord Krishna, and then they adopt a path for transitional purposes of elevation and ultimately come to Lord Krishna, then all their paths will lead to the same goal.

But if people do not share the same clear goal and they have their own conceptions . . . of their goals, then all paths will not lead to the same goal, but to different goals according to what one's individual conception is.

Q. 22

Did Lord Rama eat meat?

The word 'mamsah' is used in the Ramayana; what it refers to is certainly not decided. If we look at the overall evidence of Vedic culture, the answer would be 'no', Lord Rama did not eat meat, because vegetarianism is strongly emphasized in the Vedic. So let us look at the specific verses and context in which these references come.

Reference 1: Misconception that Sita tells Lord Rama to kill the beautiful golden deer (so that they could eat its flesh).

The assumption that Sita asks Lord Rama to kill the deer so they could eat its flesh is incorrect. The Ramayana mentions that Sita was captivated by the golden deer when she saw it grazing near their ashram in the forest. She wanted it as a pet, which she could later give to mother Kaushalya as a gift when she returned to Ayodhya. So, she did not desire the deer for its flesh. If Lord Rama had wanted to kill the deer and skin it, He would not have chased it for as long as he did. Being a famed archer, He could have shot the deer right at the beginning, as it was grazing near their ashram. But, He had to chase it because He wanted it alive as Sita did not wish to have the deer killed. As He chased the deer, it kept mystically appearing and disappearing; suddenly jumping high in the air then bounding off in another direction. When Lord Rama saw this, He understood that it was not an ordinary deer, but a demon in disguise. That was when He decided to kill it. So, the reference to meat is invalid in this context.

Reference 2: Chapter 20 of Ayodhya Kand describes Lord Rama departing for the forest, where he was to spend fourteen years in exile. In 2.20–29, Lord Rama says, 'I shall live in the solitary forest as a sage for fourteen years, living away from meat and subsisting on roots, fruits and honey.' People have thus concluded that He ate meat regularly, but would abstain from eating it while He was in the jungle. However, logically speaking, this conclusion does not make sense. Many children leave their homes to pursue their studies. When they are leaving, if they tell their parents what they shall do and what bad habits they will avoid, it does not necessarily mean that they had those habits before.

Vedic culture shows compassion for all living beings. Lord Rama goes into the forest and lives as a sage. In the forest, a person may not get enough food and in such situations, *apadharma*, which means emergency religion, can be applied. So, if it is a matter of life or death and a person has nothing else to eat and has to eat animal flesh for survival, it is accepted. It is certainly not recommended in the normal diet and certainly not for pleasure. It is quite likely that because of a lack of food, those who are living in a forest may sometimes have to resort to the eating of meat. Therefore, what Lord Rama meant was, 'Even if I have to go to the forest, I will not eat meat.' He phrases it in this manner to create emphasis. But why? Because He wants to reassure His mother Kausalya that just because He has lost His kingdom does not mean He will lose His dharma too. It is a moral reassurance that He will not lapse into immorality even though He is going into a situation where the normal protection of morality is absent.

The problem is that we want to imitate the Lord only in those things that justify our wrongdoings or support our belief system. This is due to the deep-rooted desire to gratify our senses. People who like to eat meat use these references to justify their needs as they cannot give up the habit. But they do not want to study the rest of the Ramayana to learn and apply other valuable lessons that Lord Rama has taught us. This is hypocrisy, and we must be careful not to fall prey to it.

In addition, the Lord, if He wants, can eat the whole universe (as He showed in the universal form in the Bhagavad Gita) and still be unaffected by karma, but if we try and imitate the Lord, we will only invite future suffering.

Q. 23

The Vedas say '*na tasya pratima asti*' (You are not a *pratima* or a *moorti* [idol]). Why then do we worship idols?

First and foremost, 'idol' refers to a material form. For the Lord's form, the word used is 'deity'. When the Vedas talk about pratima, they are referring to idols or a material form. They are contrasting God with material things. The form of God is not material and, in that sense, there is no material representation of Him. But there is a whole body of Vedic literature called the Pancharatras in which the concept of the God's representation in deity form is elaborated upon.

The purpose of Vedic literature is to take us from the material to the spiritual as that is our real identity. For this purpose, the Vedas talk about two paths:

1. Negation of matter for attainment of spirit
2. Use of matter as a pathway to the spirit

The Vedanta, especially the Upanishads, take the first path, the *jnana marga* or the rejection of matter, for the sake of attainment of the spirit because unless we detach from matter, we cannot advance towards the spiritual realm.

The Bhakti path, which is the conclusion of the Upanishads, is mentioned but not elaborated upon in the Upanishads. It is elaborated upon in the Itihaas and Puranas and it is clearly mentioned that although God is spiritual, we do not have to reject all matter. Matter can also be used as a pathway for the spirit and one such pathway is the deity form of God. Thus, the deity is not considered a material representation, but a spiritual manifestation. God is all powerful and He can manifest in any form, irrespective of what it is made of. So, when the scriptures talk about God being without form, they are referring to Him not having a material form.

Secondly, '*na tasya pratima asti*' also means that when we see a deity of God, we should not think that it is simply a 'moorti' or a sculptor's beautiful creation. The deity is directly God, and if we worship Him with love and devotion, He will certainly reveal Himself to us. There have been countless incidents in history where deities have spoken and had personal dealings with their devotees.

Now the question is, if the deity is God Himself, why do not we see Him in person moving about? Well, God is spiritual, and our vision is material. At the moment, all we can see is matter. Thus, God agrees to appear in a form made of matter, but this does not mean that the form is material. A deity form of God is an authorized form made on the basis of scriptures and through this, the merciful God accepts our service, which purifies us and makes us qualified to see Him in person in His original spiritual form.

In fact, the deity form is known as the *archa* incarnation of God. Every incarnation of God that appears in this world appears with a specific mission and does not act beyond it. The incarnation of Lord Narasimha appeared to protect little Prahalad, Lord Rama appeared to establish *maryada* or ideals for human society, and Lord Krishna, being the source of all incarnations, appeared to establish His supremacy. Similarly, the Lord appears as a deity with a specific mission as His name 'Archa' suggests and that is to accept the 'archana' or worship of His devotees. He makes Himself available twenty-four-seven and distributes mercy.

Thus, the verse is true: '*na tasya pratima* (idol) *asti*'. But it does not apply to the deity since the deity is not a material representation. The deity is a spiritual manifestation of Lord Krishna.

Q. 24

Is lying sinful? How can we give it up?

Yes, lying is undesirable and we should avoid it. It is considered to be one of the gravest sins. And we do it so casually.

With respect to sinfulness, it will depend on the specific lie; in what context, and for what purpose you are telling the lie. If the lie is spoken for someone's true welfare, then it is acceptable. Just like a mother who puts a pill inside a child's favourite sweet to get him to take their bitter medicine, the intention is justified. So, we have to look into our own heart and be sincere and honest, else it is a sin to lie.

In general, truthfulness is a Godly quality. In fact, it is considered to be one of the four pillars of dharma along with compassion, austerity and cleanliness.

Lord Krishna refers to truthfulness several times in the Bhagavad Gita in a positive way, and we must cultivate this quality. Now, how do we do that? In general, when we tell lies to please others, we may temporarily please them but in the long run, we lose credibility since it is very difficult to conceal lies for a long time. A few lies may be covered up, but over a period of time, when lying becomes a habit, we get caught. And even if we don't get into trouble specifically because of our lies, we are definitely in trouble when we lose our credibility. So, it is not only the future repercussions of the sin of lying, but also the immediate repercussions in terms of loss of credibility that we do not want.

How do we avoid telling lies? By deliberation and devotion.

Deliberation means we contemplate specifically or think seriously, either before or after an event. Sometimes we may blurt out an untruth but later realize that we shouldn't have spoken it. We can think about the circumstances in which we spoke a lie. Then we can plan how we can avoid telling a lie if a similar situation arises in the future.

Devotion means we pray to Lord Krishna and seek His assistance in delving deeper into the higher truths and rise above our faults such as the habit of telling lies.

On our own, we are powerless. But by the Lord's grace, we can transcend our limitations easily.

Q. 25

Why did Yudhishthir gamble? Wasn't he at fault for engaging in it and then losing everything?

There is what is known as a 'moral crisis' and then there is an 'ethical crisis'. Moral crisis means that one choice is moral whereas the other is immoral, and we have to choose between the two. For example, one is tempted to engage in a bad habit even when one knows it is bad. This is a moral crisis. The distinction in this case is clear.

An ethical crisis means that there are two options—both are ethical and both have their own morality, but one is not sure which morality to follow.

For example, let us consider a situation where there are communal riots going on and a person of a particular community is targeted by the rioters. That person comes to someone's house asking for asylum and hides in the house. Then the rioters come and ask for the person. Now, one principle is to speak the truth and another principle is to protect his life. So, what should we do? This is an ethical crisis.

Ethical crises don't have easy answers. What Yudhishthir faced was an ethical crisis.

As part of their duty, kshatriyas have to do things that are not always desirable, and Lord Krishna says this is a fact of material nature itself. 'Just as fire is covered by smoke, similarly all endeavours are covered by fault.' The fault of kshatriyas is that they often have to engage in violence. For example, they have to punish or even kill. They have to punish wrongdoers in the court of justice and sometimes kill them on the battlefield. These are difficult duties and to prepare for these, they must do certain things. For example, they must hunt to get used to the sight of blood. To develop a chivalrous spirit, they should not refuse whenever they are challenged, even if it is to gamble. That spirit is what is important. Maintaining their chivalrous spirit becomes a matter of honour for them.

Yudhishthir had been invited to gamble, but it was not so much the challenge itself that made him gamble. He could have refused it because he had more of a Brahminical nature, but he saw it more as an instruction that came from his elders. The Mahabharata tells us that Dhritarashtra wanted Yudhishthir to gamble, and it was Vidhura who brought this message to Yudhishthir. Just after the Rajasuya sacrifice, Yudhishthir had taken a vow that in order to avoid conflicts, he would always follow his elders, but he had never imagined his elders would give him such an instruction. He was initially reluctant to accept the challenge because of its implications, but he also felt that if he was challenged, he could not refuse. The challenge was one factor and the instruction of the elders was another, and thus he gambled.

Still, he could have reduced the extent of his gambling. One must accept that he did get carried away. He did not want his brothers and family to suffer. He felt that he must get all that he had lost back so they could live with dignity. Also, the wealth he had lost was meant for serving the Brahmans. 'How can I serve and maintain them without my wealth?' he thought. This was another reason he wanted to get his wealth back. Thus, his motive was neither greed nor a craving to win; it was actually a longing to serve others, and it was for this purpose that he wanted to regain all that he had lost. Unfortunately, he ended up gambling to the point of losing everything.

Life is complex, and it often presents us with ethical crises. When we are faced with one, we need an understanding of the broader purpose and priority of life so we can act accordingly.

Q. 26

If Lord Krishna is God, then how could a hunter's arrow have killed Him?

This whole world is like a stage for the Lord. A drama is meant for entertainment and teaching lessons. We do not take the events of a drama seriously as we know they are being enacted by someone who is playing a role. Similarly, whenever we consider the activities of the Lord, we must understand that He is performing pastimes or lila. As part of the lila, He does certain things that do not necessarily reflect His position as God in terms of his supremacy. When Lord Krishna becomes a charioteer for Arjuna, we must understand that he has accepted the position of the charioteer out of love for His devotee. That expresses the loving nature of God apart from His supremacy. God is not constantly doing things to prove His supremacy. He has other principles to demonstrate too and one of them is how He subordinates Himself to the love of His devotees and becomes their servant. So trying to examine every activity of the Lord through a lens of doubt will only lead us astray.

Now let us examine the episode of the arrow shot by a hunter that is described in the Mahabharata. The arrow pierced Lord Krishna's foot, and it is common knowledge that an arrow wound to a foot is not fatal, unless that arrow is poisoned. The scriptures describe this incident in such a way that the faithful are moved to maintain their faith and the doubtful will always remain in doubt. The choice is up to the individual. If we are going to accept Lord Krishna's pastimes as described in the scriptures, then we must accept all His pastimes. He even went to the abode of Yamaraj and brought back the son of Sandeepani *muni* (priest). How can a person who went to the abode of death to bring someone back succumb to death by a mere arrow wound to the foot?

The truth is, He was not even disturbed by the wound. The hunter who shot the arrow, however, was very troubled, and he came and fell at His feet, begging for forgiveness. He said, 'I thought this was the foot of an animal and that is why I shot it. Please forgive me.' Lord Krishna remained tranquil and pacified the hunter. After that, He chose to enter a trance and disappeared from the world.

The Lord comes to this world along with His associates with a specific mission to establish dharma and when it is complete, He goes back to His abode. But since He comes into the world of humans, He creates situations which appear to be human but they are not. When the Lord wanted to wind up His pastimes on this planet almost five thousand years ago, He created an entire pastime of His community of Yadus being cursed by the sages for making fun of them so that the Yadu dynasty could also end and return with Him to the spiritual world.

Once, some Yadus, in the mood to have some fun, dressed Samba, Lord Krishna's son from Jambavati, as a pregnant woman and approached the sages headed by Narada. The sages were engaged in serious discussion about the glories of the Lord. The Yadus interrupted their discussion to ask whether a boy or a girl would be born of Samba. The sages got very upset at their audacity and cursed them saying, 'Neither a boy nor a girl but an iron club will be born, which will become the cause of the destruction of the entire Yadu dynasty.'

They Yadus had descended from the spiritual realm with Lord Krishna and some of them were heavenly demigods who had come to assist Him in His mission. Now, since the Lord had completed His mission, He wished to return to His abode and wanted His associates to return too. So He arranged the return in such a way that it all looked human. Since no one else could kill them due to their immense power, Lord Krishna orchestrated that the Yadus one day got intoxicated and fought with each other with the weapons made out of the cursed iron club, a part of which was also used to fashion the tip of the arrow that the hunter shot at Him. Since the curse of the sages was on the entire Yadu dynasty and Lord Krishna identified Himself with the same, He also decided to end His pastime in the same way, and hence He made it so that He was hit by an arrow made from a part of that lethal club. Also, He wanted us to know that a sage's curse is infallible, and thus took it upon Himself as well, though no curse could affect Him. In so doing He taught us how we must be careful in dealing with people of such calibre.

If we try to apply our limited logic to the Lord's activities, we will be constantly confused because He is beyond logic. He and His activities can only be understood by grace, and grace begins where logic ends.

Q. 27

Isn't fasting an unnecessary form of self-torture?

Not at all. On the contrary, for many people, their daily overindulgence in food is unnecessary self-torture. WHO statistics show that around 1.9 billion people suffer due to obesity, whereas 690 million people suffer due to undernourishment. More health disorders are due to overeating rather than fasting. We eat more often to fulfil the greed of the mind rather than the need of the body. Due to eating too often and too much, our digestive system becomes a perpetually overworked machine in desperate need of rest. That is why many alternative medicine practitioners recommend periodic—fortnightly or monthly—fasting with intake of only fluids, so as to rest and flush the digestive system. Though abstaining from food may seem like an infliction of torture for our minds, it may well be a relief from torture for our bodies.

Fasting, when done according to scriptural guidance, can also purify the mind and lead to spiritual realization. The

Bhagavad Gita explains how we are not these material bodies, but spiritual beings or souls residing within the body. But how can we transform this intellectual understanding into an experiential realization? Fasting is one important way.

In our ordinary lives, we give in to the demands of the flesh, thus perpetuating our misidentification with the material body. Consequently, the desire to fulfil our bodily demands preoccupies and fills our minds, leaving little mental room for spiritual contemplation. When we resolve to fast on certain days, we soon realize that if we keep thinking of food while fasting, we will simply be torturing ourselves. This realization gives us the impetus to evict thoughts of food from our minds. Then, we become free to contemplate the deeper spiritual dimension of our existence, which is the goal of fasting on sacred days. Of course, such contemplation is possible without fasting too, but starving the flesh sharpens the spirit, thus making spiritual contemplation more intense. When we do not eat, we sleep less and thus the extra time created is used for cultivating our spiritual life. But if someone simply fasts and does not work towards this spiritual goal, then fasting certainly feels like torture. During the fasting period, if we lovingly call out to God by chanting His names like the Hare Krishna mahamantra, we can experience a non-material nourishment that is far more fulfilling than the most delicious food. This strengthens our realization of our spiritual identity, reinforces our commitment to the path of progressive spiritual advancement and ultimately elevates us to the realm of everlasting devotional delight. Thus, temporary bodily fasting eventually becomes a doorway to eternal spiritual feasting.

Q. 28

Why did Lord Rama banish Sita?

In reality, Lord Rama never banished Sita. Banishment would have implied being evicted from the kingdom without any arrangements for food, clothing or shelter, which is what happened to Lord Rama when he was banished by his stepmother, Kaikeyi. But in the case of Sita, she never left Lord Rama's kingdom, and He also made sure she was well taken care of. He asked Lakshmana to escort Sita to the hermitage of the sage Valmiki, where the venerable sage received her with a respectful *aarti* (worship), and the elderly lady-hermits lovingly cared for her. As the hermitage was in the kingdom of Lord Rama and under his protection, it is incorrect to say that He banished Sita, for the Lord indirectly arranged for her food, clothing, shelter and care.

Now we may ask: Why did the Lord send Sita out of His own palace into the hermitage?

To understand the answer, we need to appreciate the values held sacred by the Vedic culture that the Ramayana demonstrates. The Vedic culture considers all relationships

as opportunities for sacred service, service to God and to all
His children. When Lord Rama heard the accusations being
levelled against His consort, the situation constituted an
ethical crisis. In an ethical crisis, one has two choices, both
moral, unlike in a moral crisis, when one has two choices, one
moral and the other, immoral. To resolve an ethical crisis,
one needs profound wisdom to recognize the higher moral
principle and adjust the lower moral principle accordingly.
So, through this incident, Lord Rama, who was God
incarnate playing the role of an ideal human being, taught
us how to wisely resolve ethical crises. He had descended
into this world to set the highest standards (maryada) for all
aspects of human society. When He went to the forest in exile
despite not being obliged to do so, He was acting as an ideal
son. When He helped Sugriva regain his kingdom by killing
Vali, He acted as an ideal friend. When He crossed the ocean
to save His dear consort Sita from the mighty demon Ravana,
He acted as an ideal husband. And when He sent Sita away,
He acted as an ideal leader. An ideal leader must be above
suspicion. The duty of a leader is sacred as he is supposed to
make sure that His followers advance not only materially, but
spiritually as well. He must set the ideal standards. If people
develop suspicions about their leader for any reason, they lose
trust in the leader, and thus will not listen to or follow him.
As a leader, a person has a responsibility to a bigger family
that looks up to him. Lord Rama, through this pastime,
demonstrated how a leader must be willing to give up His
personal happiness for the sake of serving the greater family.
It was a pure act of selflessness, since no one loved Sita more

than Lord Rama, and the proof was his going all out to bring her back from the captivity of Ravana.

We must understand that the Lord played a different role on different occasions, and we must not mix those roles. Rather, we should learn the essential principles He is trying to teach us.

This whole world is a stage for the Lord. A drama is meant to achieve two things: entertain and enlighten (deliver a message).

The Lord comes into this world with His associates/ devotees from the spiritual realm, and through His interactions with them, teaches us valuable lessons. If some people fight on the stage, it does not mean that they are fighting in reality. It is simply a part of the script. If we go backstage, we will see that they are happily joking, laughing and dining with one another. Similarly, Lord Rama and His eternal consort Sita came to this world, played Their role to teach us something valuable and went back, happily reunited in the spiritual realm of Vaikuntha. But, without understanding the essence of this pastime of Sita being sent away, we will find fault with Lord Rama, thus implicating ourselves more and more in the laws of karma.

As an ideal husband, the Lord was duty-bound to protect His wife. But as an ideal king, He was also duty-bound to set an example and teach His citizens, whom He loved like His own children. Ordinarily, people are very attached to their spouse, children, home and wealth. Lord Rama considered His duty as an ideal king to be more important than His duty as an ideal husband, and so He sacrificed His love for His wife for the sake of His children (citizens). But He didn't abandon His duty as a husband; He thoughtfully performed that duty by transferring Sita from His direct care in the palace to His indirect care in the hermitage. Sita, understanding the heart of her Lord, gracefully accepted her part in his sacrifice. Unfortunately, all of us, for whose sake He made this glorious sacrifice, fail to appreciate Him.

Q. 29

What is the purpose of life?

Happiness and love are the purpose of life. No matter what we do, the practical purpose of all our activities remains happiness. And that happiness can be achieved through acquiring divine love. Let us analyse.

Whether it is the Bible or Koran or Vedic literature, all agree on the fact that we are spiritual beings and parcels of God. We belong to the spiritual realm, but by desiring to live a life independent of God, we have come to a world of matter, the world we are presently living in. To survive in this environment, we have been given a suitable body, the material body. Depending on the desires we cultivate, a particular body (out of 8.4 million species) is given to us, life after life. Along with it come the problems of old age, disease, death, miseries caused by the mind, miseries caused by others and those caused by natural disasters.

We want to be happy as the soul is pleasure-seeking, but these miseries impede our happiness time and again. In the Bhagavad Gita (8.15), Lord Krishna describes this world as '*duhkhalayam asasvatam*'—a place of misery, where everything is temporary. This is a place where misery is prominent and everything has a shelf life, and so it is not possible to be permanently happy. In the quest for eternal happiness, we have been transmigrating from one body to the other, life after life, but the quest never seems to end.

The reason? We are looking for the right thing in the wrong place. A spiritual being trying to find happiness in matter, in a temporary place, is an incompatible situation.

So if we want everlasting happiness, we need to return to the place that has it. And that is the spiritual world or Vaikuntha, where things are eternal and everything is blissful. We do not belong to the material world. We are the residents of the spiritual world and to go back to this original home of ours is the purpose of life. The human body is the best facility to accomplish this, since only humans are blessed with the facility to rectify their karma and put an end to the transmigration of the soul. How do we achieve this?

By turning to God once again through devotional service (Bhakti Yoga). Just like the process of karmic bondage begins as soon as we desire to live a life as per our whims and fancies, the process can also end as soon as we turn to Him. Karma ceases to act upon those who agree to abide by the laws of God.

Does this mean that we should not have other goals in life? No!

We certainly can have immediate goals and try our best to accomplish them, but we must do so without losing sight of the ultimate goal mentioned above. All our endeavours in life must be in line with this ultimate goal.

Most people think their goal is to eat, drink and be merry. But even animals do that—they eat, sleep, mate and defend what they have. And they are very happy doing these. If our life or happiness is also centred on these activities with no higher goal, how are we better than them?

Human life begins when we rise above these four propensities and start working towards the ultimate goal, which is spiritual.

A civilization without a spiritual culture based on scriptures is an animal civilization.

To remind us of our real goal, the Lord incarnates again and again into this world, and sends scriptures and His servants to convey His message time and again.

To conclude, the purpose of life is to put an end to the cycle of transmigration and go back to our original home where we can find everlasting happiness. This can be achieved by reviving our connection with and developing pure love for the divine Lord through the process of devotional service, primarily the chanting of His holy names:

Hare Krishna Hare Krishna Krishna Krishna Hare Hare
Hare Rama Hare Rama Rama Rama Hare Hare

If we do not realize and act accordingly, we again fall into the lower species, where we can only live our karma, but never change it.

Q. 30

How can we experience spiritual bliss?

By absorption.

If we wish to realize the power or benefit of something, we have to absorb ourselves in it. But the problem is that we are too distracted and tuned in to various frequencies at the same time. Thus, the reception of spiritual bliss is not proper.

People living in the same world see it remarkably differently: a cricket fan sees cricket everywhere, a businessman sees business everywhere and a greedy person sees money everywhere. To understand how all these different mental worlds arise among those living in the same physical world, let us consider the way a TV works. When a person tunes in to a particular channel, the TV antenna catches the corresponding vibration among the hundreds of vibrations present in the atmosphere, and the person gets absorbed in the programme being broadcast on that channel. Another person sitting in the same house may tune in to another station and get absorbed in an entirely different programme.

If we look back at our own lives, the most joyful times are generally the times when we were single-mindedly absorbed in something, be it sports, music, a hobby, work or whatever else. Distracted people seldom experience pleasure in anything. Those who are absorbed in a particular thing get a sense of pleasure from their respective absorptions. But the best pleasure comes from absorption in God. Why?

The Bhagavad Gita explains that all of us are essentially spiritual beings who belong to the spiritual realm. There, we are eternally, ecstatically absorbed in loving service to the all-attractive supreme God, Lord Krishna. When we come to this world, we seek that same ecstasy by absorbing ourselves in various worldly objects. But while God is eternal, all worldly objects are temporary. As a result, the mental worlds arising from absorption in worldly objects become temporary mental creations, whereas the mental world arising from absorption in God connects us to something permanent, the eternal spiritual realm of God, to which we actually belong. It is like a TV programme that reminds a lost child about his original home and shows him the way back.

As most of us are absorbed in everything other than God, He offers various divine tuners: the sacred books that broadcast his message of love, the holy places where he descended to reveal his world of love, the sanctified images that enable us to lovingly relate to Him as a person, and most importantly, His holy name, which gives us an intense, ecstatic experience of His loving presence. When we become devotionally absorbed in these, we too will experience supreme bliss, for we will have tuned in to the best TV (transcendental vibration).

Q. 31

What is the significance of the aarti performed in temples?

The aarti is a profound act of gratitude and selfless devotion to glorify God.

In the Bhagavad Gita (7.4) Lord Krishna explains:

bhumir apo 'nalo vayuh
kham mano buddhir eva ca
ahankara itiyam me
bhinna prakrtir astadha

'Earth, water, fire, air, ether, mind, intelligence and
false ego—together, these form My separated material
energies.'

This whole creation, including our bodies and everything we see and associate with, is made up of these eight elements only. Thus, whatever we are and whatever we use, everything belongs to the Lord, and He mercifully allows us to use it. To humbly and gratefully acknowledge this divine proprietorship of the Lord, aarti is the method prescribed in the Vedic texts such as the Pancharatras.

It signifies the offering of creation (represented by the various items offered during the aarti) back to the creator (represented by the deity, the iconic representation of the divine) as an act of gratitude: '*tera tujh ko arpan*' (what is yours is being offered to you). Since we receive so much from Him, we acknowledge it and wish to offer something in return. But because He is so great and everything is already His, we do not have anything to give. So we try to offer His own creation back to Him for His pleasure in the form of items that are symbolic of the various elements of His creation.

It is similar to a mother giving her penniless child a hundred-rupee note. He goes to the market, buys a rose, offers it to his mother and makes her immensely happy, even though the money with which the rose was bought belonged to her.

During the aarti, the various items offered to the deity represent the eight elements: the flower and the cloth represent earth, the water represents the element water, the ghee lamp represents fire, the yak-tail fan represents air, the sound of the conch and the bell represent ether, the emotional involvement in the songs sung and the mantras chanted represent the mind, the intellectual focus on the purpose of the aarti represents the intelligence, the obeisance represents the ego and the pujari represents the assembled worshippers.

All the items are offered by waving them in a circle around the deity, to remind us to keep the Lord at the centre of our activities during the cyclic motions of time, from minutes to decades.

Etymologically, the word 'aarti' means 'before night'. This refers to the fact that the first of the aartis in traditional temples is performed before the night ends, that is, at early dawn. As the dark forgetfulness of God tends to envelop us, the aarti is performed to end the night of forgetfulness.

When we reverentially observe the aarti, our mind becomes illuminated with God's glory, and our heart becomes enlivened with God's beauty. The items offered are transmuted into carriers of divine mercy or prasad, and thus we receive divine energy from the lamp's flame, the sacred water sprinkled on our bowed heads, the sanctified flowers whose fragrance we inhale.

The Vedic scriptures explain that a person who sees the face of the Lord while the aarti is being performed will have all his sinful reactions destroyed.

Q. 32

Why do we offer food to God?

Although the tradition of offering food to God before we eat is waning with the passage of time, we still see it being kept alive in many traditional families in India. But why do we need to offer it? Sometimes people argue, 'Why should we offer God food? He is God. He has everything.'

Well! Let us understand the essence and importance of the tradition at a few different levels.

1. **Gratitude:** Our meals are the times when we can most easily recognize God's grace in our lives. Of course, in our high-speed, hi-tech, fast-food lifestyle, it is not easy to remember that God is the only food producer. All our technological wizardry can only make food-processing industries, not food-producing industries. It is by God's loving master plan that mother nature transforms rains into grains. We cannot eat nuts and bolts.

   As most traditional cultures lived close to nature, they could clearly see the divine hand as the ultimate provider of their daily meals, and thus incorporated rituals for thanking God before they ate their meals. As our meals form an indispensable part of our daily schedules, no matter how busy we are, thanking God by offering mealtime prayers is a practical way of spiritualizing our daily lives. In Vedic tradition, this universal principle of spiritualizing our eating finds subtle and sophisticated expression in offering meals to God before eating them oneself, acknowledging His immense contribution.

2. **Respect:** In a cultured family, the eldest or the most respected person is offered the meal first as a sign of respect. Since we recognize God as the supreme person living in our house, He is offered everything before anyone else.

3. **Love:** If we love someone or wish to express that love, then we let that person have the first honour of enjoying the best of what we have. So offering our food to God before we eat is a sign of love, since food signifies a dear object of sense gratification and by offering it to the Lord, we are expressing that we can delay or sacrifice our pleasure to make the object of our love (God) happy. It is similar to parents sacrificing their pleasure by making sure their child eats and enjoys first.

4. **Karma-free diet:** In the Bhagavad Gita (3.13), Lord Krishna says:

> *yajna-sistasinah santo*
> *mucyante sarva-kilbisaih*
> *bhunjate te tv agham papa*
> *ye pacanty atma-karanat*

'The devotees of the Lord are released from all kinds
of sins because they eat food which is offered first for
sacrifice. Others, who prepare food for personal sense
enjoyment, verily eat only sin.'

Obviously non-vegetarian food cannot be offered to the
Lord. But even when we are offering vegetarian food,
there is some karma involved as we are destroying a life
form. Also, the energy of the person cooking also goes
into the food. This combined karma can impact our
thoughts and behaviour since we are what we eat. So if
we offer food to the Lord before we eat it, by the Lord's
mercy, the karmic energy is neutralized and the food
becomes surcharged with spiritual energy, which then
cleanses our thoughts and energy.

The Lord has promised that if anything is offered to
Him with love and devotion, He will accept it. After the
food is offered, it is known as 'prasad', which literally means
'mercy'. And when we accept this mercy, we are blessed.

So we offer food to God not because He needs it, but because
we need it, for our own well-being.

Srila Prabhupada (the Founder Acharya of ISKCON),
who popularized this tradition across the world, would say
that if even a dog eats prasad once, it will jump over all other
species in the evolutionary cycle and in its next life, it will
be born as a human being. Thus, eating food sanctified by
offering it to God can even intervene in a person's karmic
cycle and elevate him without any extra endeavour.

We must contemplate this: if a dog who doesn't even understand the power of prasad can be so elevated after eating it only once, how much benefit can we humans receive by eating such food regularly with proper consciousness?

Q. 33

Is there any scientific proof for the existence of the soul?

Yes, there is plenty of such proof. Let us consider just one category of evidence offered by near-death experiences (NDEs).

NDEs are experiences of extraordinary visions and perceptions during periods of unconsciousness among people who were medically dead or nearly dead due to various causes like accidents, disease, surgery or attempted suicide.

From the viewpoint of scientific testability, the most relevant among the NDEs are the out-of-body experiences in which the patients report having seen their body from outside it—generally from above the operating bed—and give verifiable descriptions of, say, the surgical procedures adopted by the medical staff, or of the events in their immediate vicinity or even beyond it.

Many such cases have been documented by Dr Michael Sabom, an American cardiologist who has investigated NDEs for over three decades, in his book *Recollections of Death: A Medical Investigation*. Here is one of the cases.

Sabom reports a case in which a patient recovering from sickness suffered an unexpected cardiac arrest. After he was revived, he reported that he had had an out-of-body experience in which he had travelled down the hall and seen his wife, eldest son and daughter arriving there, which was what had actually happened. This information is significant because firstly, as he was soon to be discharged, he was not expecting his family members to visit. Secondly, even if he had known that they would be visiting him, he couldn't have known who would be visiting because he had six grown children who were taking turns to accompany their mother when she came to see him. Thirdly, his family members were stopped in a hall that was ten doors away from the room where he was being worked on by the doctors and nurses. Fourthly, during their stay in the hall, his face was turned away from them, and finally, he was in the middle of being resuscitated from a cardiac arrest when they were in the hall.

Sabom's pioneering work led to hundreds of scientists all over the globe taking up NDE research under serious global forums such as the International Association for Near-Death Studies (IANDS) with peer-reviewed publications such as the *Journal of Near-Death Studies*.

In these cases, the soul moves out of the body, moves about in or slightly beyond its vicinity and returns after some time. The person does not die as it is not the destined moment for the person to die. It is similar to when we are driving downhill and we switch off the engine of our car. After some time, we switch the engine back on.

Another set of solid proof is the thousands of cases of reincarnation thoroughly researched and verified by Dr Ian Stevenson from the United States, who was assisted by a lady named Satwant Pasricha from Bengaluru in many such cases. Dr Stevenson's first book, *20 Cases Suggestive of Reincarnation*, drew a lot of attention. In it, he mentions his case studies, not based on sentiments or assumptions made by listening to a child's recollections of their past life, but on verification of facts, personal visits and eyewitnesses. And these cases are not just from India, but from all parts of the world, proving that the phenomenon of reincarnation is universal. As the Bhagavad Gita (2.13) emphatically declares:

> *dehino 'smin yatha dehe*
> *kaumaram yauvanam jara*
> *tatha dehantara-praptir*
> *dhiras tatra na muhyati*

'As the embodied soul continually passes in this body, from boyhood to youth to old age, the soul similarly passes into another body at death. The self-realized soul is not bewildered by such a change.'

Q. 34

Why do people fight in the name of religion?

Because of immaturity or selfish motives. Let us examine these more closely.

1. Immaturity: most people use religion not to *improve* themselves, but to *prove* themselves.

All of us, at our core, are spiritual beings, children of the one supreme God, and are members of the same family. Unfortunately, due to our present materialistic misconceptions, we are unable to realize this spiritual interconnectedness of all living beings. That is why God and his representatives have given the various great religions of the world as methods to cure us of this disease of materialism and to restore our original spiritual health and harmony.

The founders of the great religions have made statements saying that the way they teach is the only way. But if we study their teachings carefully, they have also made statements saying that those following other paths should be allowed to peacefully pursue their paths. How are we to reconcile these contradictory statements? The 'this is the only way' statements are meant to create a focus, a one-pointedness that can lead to wholehearted application and practical transformation. If a beginner puts his mind to too many things, he will get further confused. But if these 'only way' statements are seen as absolute, universal truths that apply at all times and in all places, then they contradict the other words of those very seers—and also defeat their ultimate purpose that others should also be allowed to practice their way.

For example, when competent doctors treat patients, they request, even insist, that their patients follow their prescribed treatment exclusively, without taking treatment from other doctors. But if the patients take such a statement to imply that all other doctors are quacks, then they miss the essential point of the doctor: to focus on their own treatment.

Those religionists who focus on applying the teachings of their founders soon advance to the spiritual level where they can see the truth in other religious paths—and thus understand the context and purpose of 'the only way' statements in their own scriptures. Therefore, here is a simple acid test for spiritual immaturity and religious fundamentalism: if the teachers and followers of a particular path stick to 'the only way' literalistic interpretation of their scriptures, then they can safely be classified as fundamentalists, who will eventually turn intolerant and even violent against those following other religions, and thus defeat the purpose of the very God in whose name they claim to be fighting.

But if the teachers and followers of a path acknowledge the truth and the validity of other paths based on objective criterion, then they have understood the essence and purpose of scriptures, and they and they alone will fulfil the purpose of God: to bring peace and harmony in this world and to lead people back to the spiritual world.

What the world needs today is sincere spiritualists who want to improve, not prove.

2. Selfish motives: religion is meant to unite and never divide.

The different religions of the world are basically different means to help us reach a common end: falling in love with God. An essential symptom of those who are attracted to God is that they lose attraction to worldly allurements like pleasures and treasures, positions and possessions. The greatest worldly allurement is the allurement of the ego, which unrelentingly impels us to think of ourselves as superior to others. Those who love God cherish no love for their egos; for them, proving the superiority of their own path holds far less importance than treading that path and increasing their own love for God—and inspiring others to do the same. Such saintly people are adorned by the qualities that make a person lovable and loving among one and all: humility, gentleness, helpfulness, tolerance, selflessness and compassion.

Far removed from such saints are those who use their religious faith as a means, not to transcend, but to feed their egos. For them, their religion is not a means to increase their connection to God, but a means to prove their own superiority over others: 'My religion is better than yours, and so I am better than you.' No wonder such people don't hesitate to fight in the name of their religion; indeed, they often consider it their religious duty to engage in such fights. But this duty is not to the religion of God, but to the religion of the ego. Just as the ego incites people to fight in the name of race, caste, gender and nationality, similarly, it instigates people to fight in the name of religion.

Certain individuals exploit the religious sentiments of people to carry out their own personal agendas, since most people have a very emotional connection with religion. And those who are vulnerable with regard to something are easy prey to those who know how to exploit and incite.

Often when people say, 'My God or my way is the best', it is not as much about their 'way' or 'God' or a particular deity they claim to worship as it is about their own egos. 'Mine is the best.' Why? 'Because I am the best.' This is a subtle message and has a hidden meaning in it.

To do away with this, we need thorough education about what true religion is all about, what its goal is and how to pursue it. Unless we recognize that we have a common universal father, we will never have universal brotherhood.

Hindu, Muslim, Christian, Sikh or Jain are all external designations and these can change. Today, someone who is a Hindu and fighting against Muslims might be reborn as a Muslim in the next life and vice versa. A Jain might become a Sikh in the next life and so on. We have a short lifespan, but we keep fighting in the name of God. Do we think our

God will be happy? Which father would be happy seeing his children fighting?

We need to grow up. Any religious faith that considers itself superior and demeans others is a manifestation of deep-rooted hypocrisy. We are not pleasing God with this attitude. Rather, we are giving Him immense pain.

We must follow our path and at the same time, respect others' paths too and allow them to evolve as per their understanding. Everyone is at a different level and must be respected, thus avoiding the narrow-minded and sentimental approach.

Q. 35

If God has designed our world, then why is there so much suffering here?

Everything within the Lord's creation has a specific purpose. God is eternally kind and His kindness manifests at various levels in different ways. But if He is so kind, why has He created such a messy world?

Well! We must understand this from the following example. The government plans a nice city replete with all kinds of facilities such as stadiums, parks, hospitals, roads, educational institutions, shopping malls, and one more important thing—the prison. And what happens inside a prison? Criminals are punished. But why? To rectify their wrong behaviour. So why does the government have to build a messy place like a prison? The answer is simple. The government designs all the facilities for the welfare of the citizens. There are certain laws that everyone is expected to abide by to maintain peace and harmony in the city. However, it is also expected that some citizens, misusing their free will, will break the laws and create disorder, disturbing the harmonious atmosphere in the city. To protect others, such people cannot be allowed to move around freely, and a special place needs to be designated for them to rectify their wrong mentality. That is the prison.

Similarly, the Vedic scriptures explain that we are spiritual beings, residents of the spiritual world where we live in peace and harmony with the will of the Lord. Being His parts and parcels, we are also endowed with something called 'free will'. When we misuse our free will and try to live a life independent of God by developing independent or material desires, it disturbs the harmony of the spiritual realm, and a separate place needs to be created for all of us for two reasons:

1. To allow us a facility where we can fulfil our desires
2. To rectify our wrong attitude

To fulfil desires, there are 8.4 million types of bodies, just as we have different types of garments for various occasions. But simultaneously, the Lord also creates various miseries in proportion to our wrong mentality and activities, so we don't take things for granted and we rectify our consciousness; because if a person who commits a crime is not punished, he will keep doing it, and thus keep suffering. To keep a check on us, miseries are essential, so we realize our mistakes and start cooperating with His will, just as speed breakers are important to keep a check on speeding vehicles.

So God did not need to create this messy place. We forced Him to. The government will not need a prison if everyone becomes a law-abiding citizen. So if we also begin to cooperate with His will, which is mentioned in the scriptures such as the Bhagavad Gita and Srimad Bhagavatam, then this messy world would cease to exist.

In fact, if we start living our life as per the Lord's will, even in this world, we can experience great ecstasy.

And what is His will?

He explains in the Bhagavad Gita (18.65):

man-mana bhava mad-bhakto
mad-yaji mam namaskuru
mam evaisyasi satyam te
pratijane priyo 'si me

'Always think of Me and become My devotee. Worship
Me and offer your homage unto Me. Thus, you will
come to Me without fail. I promise you this because you
are My very dear friend.'

Also, miseries exist so that one day we get fed up with this world and question, 'Is there a better place than this where I do not have to go through so much? How can I get out of here?' As soon as we start questioning like this, we must know that our journey back home, where we actually belong, has already begun. The Lord seated in our heart as Parmatma will guide us to the right sources and resources.

A life of misery begins when we turn away from Him, and it will end as we turn to Him. We are suffering because of our own wrong desires, but we can get rid of our suffering by once again rightly directing our desires.

Q. 36

What is the role of logic on the spiritual path?

On the spiritual path, we can and should use our logical faculty, but we should also not stay stuck in logic; we should progress from logic to experience based on the experience of those who have already conducted the experiment. In schools and colleges, we do not always use logic or even if we do, we do not remain stuck. Either we accept what is being taught, trusting the teacher, or we experiment to verify something ourselves. We must accept the fact that we are imperfect and thus need constant guidance from a higher intelligence.

The Vedic texts explain that presently all of us are spiritually ill. When we are spiritually healthy, we experience the peace, power and pleasure that are natural to us as eternal souls, as beloved children of the Supreme Lord. Just as the proper medical treatment can restore our bodily health, the proper spiritual practices such as hearing from the scriptures like the Bhagavad Gita, Ramayana, Mahabharata and Srimad Bhagavatam and chanting the Lord's holy names can restore our spiritual health.

Using the treatment analogy, let us see what logic can and cannot do.

What logic can do:

1. Using our logic, we can evaluate the various treatment options available to us and choose the best treatment. Similarly, logic can help us evaluate the various spiritual paths available to us and choose as per the scriptures, the practice of chanting as the easiest, safest and fastest path to spiritual recovery.

2. Just as logic can help us systematically observe the effects of a treatment and notice when the promised results appear, it can also assist us in observing the effects of chanting on our consciousness and notice our mind becoming peaceful, pure, positive and pleasant.

What logic cannot do:

1. Just as one's health cannot be restored just by logically analysing the diagnosis, our spiritual health cannot be restored merely by analysing Vedic philosophy.

2. Just as logic cannot be a substitute for treatment, mere expertise in logical gymnastics cannot replace the actual experience of chanting.

So we must advance from the stage of logic to that of experimenting.

Blind acceptance is bad, but equally bad is blind rejection.

Thus, logic will enable us to recognize that a particular spiritual path or process is a profound and practical science—provided we are open-minded enough to experiment. Unfortunately, many people refuse to conduct the experiment, claiming in advance that it is illogical. Aren't they like judges who declare the defendant to be a criminal without even hearing the case? They may claim to be champions of logic, but aren't they themselves being illogical? Logic is a precious tool for discerning the truth, but sadly, for such people, logic becomes a trap that keeps them in self-imposed and self-righteous misunderstanding.

Thus, on the spiritual path, logic is necessary but not sufficient. Therefore, let us combine our head's logic with our heart's experience to examine spirituality by the application of what we hear from the scriptures.

Q. 37

When God is one, why does the Vedic tradition teach the worship of many gods?

God is the supreme being and He is a single entity. There is no doubt about it. In fact, there will be no confusion in our minds if we study the scriptures.

The many Gods of the Vedic tradition are like various departmental heads in the universal government of God.

In an organization, we have the chief executive officer, the chief financial officer, the head of human resources and so on. Similarly, within the universe, many departments have been identified that need supervision. Some of these are the departments of rain, education, finance, fire, heat, light, construction, justice and so on. To handle these, He has appointed various qualified individuals. For rain, we have Indra in charge. For heat, there is Agni. For light, we have the Sun. For education, Goddess Saraswati, for construction Lord Brahma and for justice, Yamraj, also known as Lord Dharmraj.

All these demigods are endowed with special powers to run universal affairs. They are created at the beginning

of creation itself as described by the Supreme Lord in the
Bhagavad Gita (3.10):

saha-yajnah prajah srstva
purovaca prajapatih
anena prasavisyadhvam
esa vo 'stv ista-kama-dhuk

'In the beginning of creation, the Lord of all creatures
sent forth generations of men and demigods, along
with sacrifices for Vishnu, and blessed them by saying,
"Be thou happy by this yajna [sacrifice] because its
performance will bestow upon you all desirable things."'

Why are they created?

1. **To provide for our needs:** Rebellious souls like us
   who want to live separate from God are sent into this
   material world to fulfil personal desires. However, like
   a loving father who still makes arrangements for the
   subsistence of a son who has rebelled against him and left
   His association, the Supreme Lord Krishna also makes
   similar arrangements by appointing qualified individuals
   to facilitate our needs in exchange for the *yajnas* (fire
   sacrifices) we are expected to perform to honour them (as
   mentioned in the verse above).

   These demigods are like us, but with heaps and heaps
   of pious activities.

2. **To gradually elevate us:** Those who are disconnected from God and only motivated by their desires learn about demigods who can facilitate that fulfilment to some extent. Thus, they start worshiping them. But in the process of worship as per the Vedic rituals in the scriptures, three important things happen:

   1) They get connected to God indirectly as demigods are His agents.

   2) They are gradually purified due to the power of the Vedic process of worship.

   3) In the process, they hear about a higher reality than them and about how life should not simply be centred on 'I, me and mine'. We must learn to make God, who is the master and well-wisher of everyone, the centre of our life.

Thus, the demigods act to connect the disconnected to the Supreme Lord, but in an indirect way, as all the benefits they bestow are bestowed after Lord Krishna's sanction.

Lord Krishna describes this extraordinary system in the Bhagavad Gita (7.20-23): 'Those whose intelligence has been stolen by material desires surrender unto demigods and follow the particular rules and regulations of worship according to their own natures. As soon as one desires to worship some demigod, I make his faith steady so that he can devote himself to that particular deity. Endowed with such a faith, he endeavours to worship a particular demigod and obtains his desires. But in actuality these benefits are bestowed by Me alone.'

Thus, there is only one God and others are demigods working under his supreme direction to carry out the universal affairs for the benefit of those who are stuck in the material world.

Q. 38

Why do you consider Lord Krishna to be God?

Because the scriptures and great authorities of the past say so.

All our information about God must be substantiated by scriptural references and by teachers who teach from scriptures. The Vedic scriptures are the only scriptures that have existed since the beginning of time, and thus are the absolute truth. There is no higher authority than that of the Vedic scriptures.

They give us an objective description of God as the person possessing the six excellences: wealth, strength, wisdom, beauty, fame and renunciation. People are attracted to anyone who possesses even a fraction of one of these. And Lord Krishna literally means, 'the all-attractive'.

No wonder Lord Krishna is celebrated in Vedic tradition as God in His highest manifestation, as the epitome of all-attractiveness.

Yes, God is all-powerful and all-merciful as indicated by names such as Allah and Jehovah, but his all-powerfulness and his all-mercifulness contribute to making him all-attractive.

And his all-attractiveness includes every other divine attribute like all-powerfulness and all-mercifulness.

Still, some may consider Lord Krishna to be a sectarian God worshipped by a particular tradition. However, in principle, the Vedic revelation of Lord Krishna doesn't *contradict* the revelations of God in other religious traditions. But none of the great theistic religions would deny that God possesses the six excellences. Significantly, these traditions don't reveal any personality who possesses them as the teachings are given as per the calibre of the students, else they might reject the teacher himself. To the neophyte, basic instructions are given and to the advanced ones, advanced instructions are given.

In fact, many Vedic books do not reveal His name because even Vedic tradition acknowledges the fact that there are different individuals at different levels of understanding, that they must be given only as much as they can digest. Only a few advanced scriptures such as the Bhagavad Gita, Srimad Bhagavatam and a few puranas reveal the true identity of that one supreme person.

Bhagavad Gita literally means 'Song of God'. And we all know who has sung that song: Lord Krishna.

In fact, Lord Krishna Himself declares that He is the Supreme Lord. If we search the entire body of Vedic literature and even world literature, no one else has made this claim.

Some references from the Bhagavad Gita:

'It should be understood that all species of life, O son of Kunti, are made possible by birth in this material nature, and that I am the seed-giving father.' (Lord Krishna, Bhagavad Gita 14.4)

'I am the father of this universe, the mother, the support and the grandsire.' (Lord Krishna, Bhagavad Gita 9.17)

'The whole cosmic order is under Me. By My will it is manifested again and again, and by My will it is annihilated at the end.' (Lord Krishna, Bhagavad Gita 9.8)

'Furthermore, O Arjuna, I am the generating seed of all existences. There is no being, moving or unmoving, that can exist without Me.' (Lord Krishna, Bhagavad Gita 10.39)

'I am the source of all spiritual and material worlds. Everything emanates from Me. The wise who perfectly know this engage in My devotional service and worship Me with all their hearts.' (Lord Krishna, Bhagavad Gita 10.8)

'Of all that is material and all that is spiritual in this world, know for certain that I am both the origin and the dissolution.' (Lord Krishna, Bhagavad Gita 7.6)

'I give heat, and I withhold and send forth the rain.' (Lord Krishna, Bhagavad Gita 9.19)

'With a single fragment of myself I pervade and support this entire universe.' (Lord Krishna, Bhagavad Gita 10.42)

'The splendour of the sun, which dissipates the darkness of the whole world, comes from Me. And the splendour of the moon and the splendour of fire are also from Me.' (Lord Krishna, Bhagavad Gita 15.12)

'I enter into each planet, and by my energy they stay in orbit.' (Lord Krishna, Bhagavad Gita 15.13)

'This material nature, which is one of My energies, is working under My direction.' (Lord Krishna, Bhagavad Gita 9.10)

'I am the super soul, O Arjuna, seated in the hearts of all living entities, I am the beginning, the middle, and the end of all beings.' (Lord Krishna, Bhagavad Gita 10.20)

'There is no truth beyond Me. Everything rests upon Me, as pearls are strung on a thread.' (Lord Krishna, Bhagavad Gita 7.7)

'O Arjuna, I know everything that has happened in the past, all that is happening in the present, and all things that are yet to come. I also know all living entities.' (Lord Krishna, Bhagavad Gita 7.26)

'Many, many births both you and I have passed. I can remember all of them, but you cannot!' (Lord Krishna, Bhagavad Gita 4.5)

'Those who are devotees of other Gods and who worship them with faith actually worship only me, O son of Kunti, but they do so in a wrong way. I am the only enjoyer and master of all sacrifices. Therefore, those who do not recognize My true transcendental nature fall down.' (Lord Krishna, Bhagavad Gita 9.24)

References from other scriptures:

Lord Brahma, who is the first created living being, states in the Brahma Samhita:

'Krishna, who is known as Govinda, is the supreme godhead. He has an eternal blissful spiritual body. He is the origin of all. He has no other origin, and He is the prime cause of all causes.' (Brahma Samhita 5.1)

After describing various incarnations of the Lord such as Rama, Balrama, Vamana, Narsimha and Vishnu, Sukadeva Goswami states:

'All of the above-mentioned incarnations are either plenary portions or portions of the plenary portions of the Lord, but Lord Krishna is the original Personality of Godhead.' (Srimad Bhagavatam 1.3.28)

Lord Shiva in the Gita Mahatmya states:

'Only one God—Krishna, the son of Devaki.' (Verse 7)

In the Padma Purana it is stated:

'By carefully reviewing all the revealed scriptures and judging them again and again, it is now concluded that Lord Narayana is the supreme absolute truth, and thus he alone should be worshipped.'

The Skanda Purana states:

'In the material world, which is full of darkness and dangers, combined with birth and death and full of different anxieties, the only way to get out of the great entanglement is to accept loving transcendental devotional service to Lord Vasudeva.'

The position of Krishna as God is confirmed by great personalities such as Narada, Asita, Devala, Parasara, Brahma and Shiva.

Also in the scriptures, we find that whenever any personality speaks, their name is mentioned. For example, when Indra speaks, it is mentioned, 'Indra Uvacha', which means, 'Indra spoke.' When Shiva speaks, it says 'Rudra

Uvacha' and so on. But whenever Lord Krishna or any of His incarnations speak, their names are not mentioned. Rather it mentions, 'Shri Bhagavan Uvacha' which means 'God spoke'. So even common sense can prove Lord Krishna's supremacy over all others.

Q. 39

Doesn't spirituality demand blind faith?

No, spirituality does not ask for blind faith, but 'reasonable faith'.

Reasonable faith means, 'I have heard about something. So let me try it. If it does not work, I can always give it up.'

Blind faith means, 'I have heard about something, but I immediately reject it without verifying it.'

Blind acceptance is bad, but blind rejection is equally bad. In fact, it is worse because we might miss out on a rare diamond, considering it to be a broken piece of glass.

Reasonable faith is not something new. If we carefully examine our daily routine, we will find that we have been applying it in every aspect of life. In fact, our life starts with reasonable faith. When we are born, we do not know who our father is. We hear who he is from our mother, and we trust her. Now if we talk about blind faith, then isn't this also blind faith because we have no direct evidence to prove it? Not at all. This is called reasonable faith because we are hearing from a reliable source. If we want, we can do a DNA test to verify it.

When we get into a cab, we don't check whether the driver has a licence and knows how to drive. We have faith that he will take us to our destination.

We go to hotels and restaurants after hearing that the food at a particular place is good. We go and try it and then come to a conclusion regarding it based on our findings. We believe that the food is not contaminated, although chances are that it could be. But we have faith.

The point is that we cannot move even an inch forward without this faith, else we will live in constant fear and go insane.

The best way to move forward is to have a certain degree of faith in everything despite it all. It is reasonable, since we cannot keep checking everything.

The same logic applies to spiritual life as well. We can hear from the right authority and move forward thinking, 'If someone is teaching something, let me try and apply it in my life and test its authenticity.'

Sometimes some people reject spiritual truths as bogus or illogical, saying they are students of science. However, they are not scientific at all because science also says that before we accept or reject a theory, it must go through six steps: aim, apparatus, theory, observation, calculation and conclusion. Only when we have tested a theory do we have the right to decide whether it is real or not.

Thus, just as we apply reasonable faith to everything in life without immediately rejecting it, spiritual life must not be an exception. We can apply the principles mentioned in the scriptures and see if they work. If they do not, give them up. But giving up without trying is unscientific and illogical.

The proof of the pudding is in the eating.

When we experiment based on what we hear, we get realizations, and those realizations increase our faith. Spiritual life requires the same logic of faith that we apply everywhere else in our life.

Q. 40

Even though Ravana kidnapped Sita, he never used force on her. Was he not a gentleman then?

Many so-called broad-minded followers of the religious tradition proclaim that Ravana was a great personality and a moral being because even though he abducted Sita and kept her in captivity for a long time, he did not even touch her or try to force himself upon her. However, the fake veil of his gentlemanly behaviour is lifted when he comes in disguise and abducts Sita when Lord Rama is away.

The scriptures describe six types of aggressors, and such people deserve the most severe punishment by the law. There is no sin incurred by inflicting punishment on them, according to the codes of conduct of dharma.

The six aggressors are: 1) one who sets fire to the house; 2) one who attacks with deadly weapons; 3) one who administers poison; 4) one who steals someone's property;

5) one who steal someone's wealth; and 6) one who kidnaps someone's wife.

According to dharma, then, Ravana was a criminal, not a gentleman.

As far as his not touching Sita even though she was in his captivity for such a long time, it was not a show of his gentlemanly behaviour, but rather a fear for his life.

He could not touch Sita, although he wanted to. There is a conversation in the Ramayana where his minister tells him, 'Why don't you molest her using force? What is stopping you?'

Ravana says, 'I want to, but I cannot because there is a curse on my head.'

And what was that curse?

Ravana, after acquiring powers from Lord Brahma, went on a rampage across the three worlds, capturing territories, killing innocent people and kidnapping and molesting women. There was not a sin that he did not commit.

Once, when he went to the heavens and was scaring its inhabitants, he saw one of the most beautiful damsels of the heavens named Rambha. He was infatuated with her and wanted to possess her, even though she happened to be the wife of his nephew, Nalakuvar, who was the son of Kuver, Ravana's cousin.

When Rambha tried to run away, Ravana ran after her and molested her. When Nalakuvar came to know of this, he was helpless and devastated, but knew he couldn't do much against the mighty demon. So he cursed him such that in the future, the demon could not repeat such an act.

He pronounced, 'If Ravana ever again tries to forcefully touch another woman against her will, his head will crack into thousand pieces, and he will fall down dead.'

Ravana knew that the curses of the celestials worked, and he remembered this one well. Thus, he could not force himself upon Sita, even though he wished to.

Q. 41

Is the law of karma scientific?

Yes and no. 'Yes' in the sense that the law of karma (for every action, there is an equal and corresponding reaction) is like the other laws of nature discovered by modern science, a foundational principle governing the world we live in. 'No' in the sense that it involves the interaction of non-quantifiable parameters such as consciousness, free will and motivation, which are beyond the realm of science.

Science has discovered that nature obeys laws for any interaction of any kind from the microscopic level to the macroscopic level. In fact, classical physics is nothing but the study and application of nature's laws. If laws govern all of nature, wouldn't it be patently unscientific to claim that humans alone are the law-exempt odd man out? Of course, humans have subtle endowments such as consciousness and free will, which insentient matter doesn't have and which are beyond the capacity of classical physics to precisely discern, quantify and explain. However, does the inability of classical physics to explain a phenomenon automatically make that phenomenon non-existent or unscientific? The reality of consciousness is undeniable; all of us know it as a self-experienced reality. Even sceptics who deny the existence of consciousness are able to deny it because they are conscious.

And truly, science means to know things as they are. We can see that if we sow a mango seed, a mango tree grows out of it. This is scientific and the law of karma also states that as we sow, so shall we reap. So yes, the law of karma is scientific and beyond science as well because it is difficult to understand how a little seed becomes a huge tree without the presence and direction of some unseen power. We must accept the fact that science has limitations and just because something cannot be proved by it does not mean it is not true. We are like frogs in the well, who, having spent all our lives inside the well, have concluded that there is nothing beyond the well. This springs from the deep-rooted pride that makes one feel that they are the centre of the universe. With our limited and imperfect senses, we can never really understand the perfect creation of the Lord and the supremely perfect laws governing it.

Q. 42

What is the need for rituals? Is it not enough to just think of God?

Rituals are the essential external means to think of and express gratitude to God. They are vehicles that connect our consciousness to the supreme.

Imagine, if someone keeps telling us, 'I love you, I love you,' but sits in one place and does nothing else! When we ask the person to get us a glass of water, the person says 'No,' but continues to say that he loves us. Is that not hypocrisy? It certainly is. If we feel love for someone, why not express it through our actions? After all, actions speak louder than words, and certainly louder than thoughts.

And if we feel bored by or apprehensive about rituals, we must understand that they are not just restricted to religion; they pervade all fields of life. Let us consider two worldly examples:

1. When we meet a stranger, the ritual of extending our hand and saying, 'I'm pleased to meet you,' gives tangible,

    recognizable and appreciable form to our desire to express cordiality and warmth.

2. On a birthday, the ritual of blowing out a candle and cutting a cake brings structure and verve to the celebration.

Many people would find a birthday celebration incomplete without candle-blowing, although candle-blowing has no intrinsic connection with a birthday. If the ritual were intrinsically connected with the essence of an occasion, then how much more would it be necessary on that occasion? For example, bowing or kneeling in a holy place is a ritual to express our humility in the presence of the divine. Could we experience the same profound humility if we were to sit leaning back in an easy chair, head resting on the palm of the hand? Arguably not.

Does not the offering of incense, flowers or a candle make us more conscious of the divine than when we are simply sitting on a couch pretending to be thinking of the Lord within? Certainly it does!

So what is the precise connection of the outer ritual with the inner essence? There is a dual connection: rituals are the means to both *express* the essence and *experience* the essence. The handshake helps express the essence of cordiality, the candle-blowing helps experience the essence of happiness, and the bowing helps both express and experience the essence of humility.

Let us now consider another ritual: the repeated chanting of the names of God. The theistic wisdom-traditions of the world declare that God extends His presence to us through His holy names. For those with devotion for God, chanting His names is the ritual to express their devotion for Him and for those who don't yet have that devotion, chanting is the ritual to experience that devotion. Those who do away with the external ritual of chanting run the risk of making their attempts to internally think of God self-congratulatory and hallucinatory because they will not experience any devotion.

And to be honest, it is very difficult to think of God internally without sincerely engaging in some spiritual practices externally. First the body must be engaged, then the heart will follow. It does not happen without an external effort.

Why do some people want to do away with rituals altogether?

Often, they are disillusioned with rituals due to seeing them enacted perfunctorily, without true devotion. Nowadays rituals have become like an empty bullet. There is a lot of noise, but no effect. The essence is lost. However, their blanket rejection of rituals generally backfires on them; it minimizes their access to the essence to a merely conceptual or superficial level.

Many times, people do not wish to engage in rituals because they do not want to. They use the excuse of 'thinking of God' within their minds (the same turbulent, distracted mind on which we have no control).

How then can we reach the essence and rectify the situation? By educating ourselves about:

1. What the essence is
2. What the connection between the ritual and the essence is
3. What the principles and techniques for connecting the ritual with the essence are

By such systematic education, we will soon experience that the rituals are synonymous and synchronous with the essence of heartfelt devotion.

Always thinking of the Lord within the heart is the essential goal, but anyone who says that he has reached or hopes to reach that stage without following rituals is only being ignorant. It is like saying we earned a PhD degree without studying.

So we have to look into our own hearts and find out why we want to avoid engaging in rituals; is it due to indifference or a distaste for rituals? Is it because we are too lazy or find them boring? If the answer to any of these questions is yes, then we better work on rectifying our mentality because rituals are also a way to say 'thank you' to the Lord who has blessed us with all that we have, including our intelligence. And instead of using that intelligence to connect with Him, we are using it to defy serving Him through the sacred science of rituals.

To love means to serve. If we truly feel love for him within our heart, we must express it through *sewa* or service (rituals).

Q. 43

If God exists, why can't we see Him?

All of us can see God, but we need the appropriate apparatus and method, just as we need a telescope to see a distant celestial object.

There is oil in oil seeds, but can we see it with our naked eye? No!

There is sugar in sugarcane, but can we see it with the naked eye? No!

There is ghee in milk, but can we see it with our present vision? No!

But through specific processes, these things can be seen.

Similarly, God is there within His creation and through a process, He can be seen as well. But the process to see material things and the process to see God differ, since God is spiritual. At the moment our eyes are material and thus, with these we cannot perceive Him. He is known as *Adhokshaja*—the one who is beyond material senses. Someone who is beyond material senses cannot be seen with material senses.

Take for example the three main branches of science, namely, physics, chemistry and biology.

1. Physics: To measure the corner of a table, we use Vernier calipers.
2. Chemistry: To check the acidity or the alkalinity of a substance, we use a litmus paper.
3. Biology: To see a microorganism, we use a microscope.

Now, can we use a microscope to check the acidity of a substance? No!

Can we use the litmus test to measure the corner of a table? No!

Can we use the Vernier calipers to see a microorganism? No!

So even in material science, the methods and the apparatus are not interchangeable. How then can we use something from within material science to understand that which is spiritual or antimatter (God)? The method and the apparatus to see God must be different.

So what is the apparatus?

Eyes full of love.

Lord Brahma explains in the Brahma Samhita (5.38):

premanjana-cchurita-bhakti- vilochanena

'Anyone whose eyes are anointed with the ointment of
love can see Him everywhere.'

And what is the method to develop that love?

Lord Krishna Himself explains in the Bhagavad Gita (18.55):

> *bhaktya mam abhijanati*
> *yavan yas casmi tattvatah*
> *tato mam tattvato jnatva*
> *visate tad-anantaram*

'One can understand Me as I am, as the Supreme
Personality of Godhead, only by devotional service.
And when one is in full consciousness of Me by such
devotion, he can enter into the kingdom of God.'

Here He clearly mentions Bhakti Yoga (*bhaktya*) as a path to
know and see Him. Not karma, dhyan or *jnana*, but bhakti.

Bhakti or devotional service begins with the process
of hearing and chanting of His name, fame, glories and
pastimes from scriptures such as the Bhagavad Gita, Srimad
Bhagavatam, Ramayana and Mahabharata. By engaging in
these activities, we gradually spiritualize our senses, with
which we then become qualified to see Him.

Without rendering devotional service, it is impossible to
approach him. If we wish to see a great personality, more
than us wanting to see him, he should also agree to see us.

For example, if we wish to have a personal audience with
the prime minister of a country, our desire is all right but
most importantly, the prime minister must also be willing to
meet us. And he will meet us if we are qualified to meet him.

Jimmy Carter was the thirty-ninth President of the United States. After he was elected as President, he was going through the newspapers to see the coverage of his election campaign. His gaze fell upon an interesting image in one of the newspapers. There was a group of Hare Krishna devotees doing kirtan on the street and among them was a man in civilian clothes. He held a board in his hand that read, 'Vote for Jimmy Carter'. This really amused the President, and he told his men that he wanted to have lunch with this person in the White House the next day.

Nobody knew who this person was, but sure enough, they found him. The very next day, this person was sitting in the White House, having lunch with the President of the United States. On his own, if he had ever wanted to come and see the President, what was the probability that he would have been able to do so? Almost negligible! But when the President wanted to see him, it happened so easily.

And why did the President want to see him? Because he was pleased with this gentleman's service. Similarly, when God is pleased with our sewa or service, He will reveal Himself. And only when He, out of His sweet will, reveals Himself, can we see Him. We cannot force Him to appear in front of us, just like we cannot force the sun to appear as and when we want. The sun appears on its own at its own timing.

We must always remember that we cannot barge into the spiritual realm. We need to qualify ourselves and enter by invitation only. Thus, we should simply try and engage in His sewa. And one day, when he is pleased, He will show Himself.

One of the greatest saints in history, Srila Bhaktisiddhanta Saraswati Thakkur, very rightly said, 'Do not try to see God. Try to serve Him in such a way that He wants to see you.'

When we want to see Him, there will be many impediments. But when He wants to see us, who can stop Him?

Q. 44

Is there any proof of reincarnation?

Certainly, there is a lot of proof of reincarnation.

We have three bodies:

1. The gross body or the outer covering that all of us can see.
2. The subtle body, consisting of subtle elements such as the mind, intelligence and false ego.
3. The soul or the spiritual body, which means us residing within the body.

At the time of death, the soul, along with the subtle body, goes to the next gross body, leaving the present gross body behind. As the same subtle body carries on to the next life, aspects related to the subtle body—skills, fears and memories—are carried from this life to the next, along with, of course, the devotional experiences associated with the soul. Whether the aspects related to the subtle body will be remembered in the next life or not will depend on the extent of impressions that have been created in the mind by the activities related to them.

Here are examples of phenomena that persuasively point to reincarnation:

- Precocious children who have abilities far beyond their years are a medical mystery. How does a child of five solve complex calculus problems that graduate-level students struggle with? Because he cultivated maths skills in his previous life.

- Many people with mental problems—especially phobias—that are incurable by normal psychotherapy have been cured by Dr Brian Weiss of the Sinai Medical Research Center in the United States. Through hypnotically-induced past life regression, he has been able to determine that these phobias originate in a traumatic previous-life death caused by the very object toward which one has a phobia in this life. For example, he found that several patients with hydrophobia had died by drowning in a previous life. When the patients understand the cause of the phobia, their phobia disappears or at least decreases dramatically. Those who don't consider reincarnation real have no explanation for the healing that has taken place.

- Numerous cases of past life memories have been documented by rigorous researchers such as Dr Ian Stevenson in his books, especially, *Where Reincarnation and Biology Intersect*. The quality of Dr Stevenson's research was acknowledged in the prestigious *Journal of the American Medical Association*: '[Dr Stevenson had] painstakingly and unemotionally collected a detailed series of cases in which the evidence for reincarnation is difficult to understand on any other grounds . . . He has placed on record a large amount of data that cannot be ignored.'

Considering these multiple proofs, it is no wonder that author Collin Watson asserted, 'The sheer volume of evidence for survival after death is so immense, that to ignore it is like standing at the foot of Mt Everest and insisting that you cannot see the mountain.'

Q. 45

Aren't yajnas, in which grains and ghee are poured into a fire, a foolish waste of money?

Yajnas will appear to be a waste only as long as we are uninformed.

Lord Krishna explains the purpose of a yajna in the Bhagavad Gita (3.10):

saha-yajnah prajah srstva
purovaca prajapatih
anena prasavisyadhvam
esa vo 'stv ista-kama-dhuk

'In the beginning of creation, the Lord of all creatures sent forth generations of men and demigods, along with yajnas, and blessed them by saying, "Be thou happy by this yajña [sacrifice] because its performance will bestow upon you everything desirable for living happily and achieving liberation."'

The Supreme Lord Himself created this system of yajnas at the beginning of creation to facilitate the fulfilment of our basic needs in the world. When we perform yajnas, we are supplied in return with the necessities of life and thus live happily in this world (as mentioned in the verse above).

While living in a country we are duty-bound to pay taxes for the facilities provided by the national government. Similarly, while living in the universe, we are expected to pay cosmic taxes for the utilities provided through nature by the cosmic government headed by God. It also happens to be an act of gratitude for whatever we receive.

The utilities of food, water, air, lumber, rocks, metals, jewels, oil and so forth lead to a staggering 'bill to nature' of $16 trillion to $54 trillion per annum, as described in *Nature* [15 May 1997].

The medium of economic exchange is known to vary greatly in accordance with the prevailing sociocultural setting. For example, if an ancient man from the Vedic age is transported through time to our society, he will be aghast to see the amount of value we ascribe to the pieces of paper we call currency notes. Just as our medium of exchange—currency notes—is unintelligible to an ancient, the Vedic medium of intra-universal exchange—sanctified fire and sound in the form of yajnas—is incomprehensible to us. An intelligent person focuses not on the medium of exchange, but the principle. Modern society gives us valuable things—time and energy—to get money. We get important things—the necessities of life—by giving money. Similarly, Vedic followers offer oblations into the sacred fire to satisfy the Cosmic Controller, and in return, receive all the gifts of nature.

The proof of the pudding is in the eating; the proof of the authenticity of the yajnas is in the resulting prosperity. The prosperity of ancient India is well known, as described both in Vedic literature such as the Srimad Bhagavatam as well as by many historians including A.L. Basham in his book, *The Wonder That Was India*. Indeed, the present world's most prosperous nation, the United States, was discovered when explorers were searching for new navigational routes to tap the prosperity of India! The principle of cosmic governance is also evident through the present erratic supply of natural resources due to our non-remittance of our cosmic tax. We see so much drought, famine, shortage of resources etc. because we are not paying our cosmic taxes. While living in a city, when we stop paying bills to the municipality, the supply of water and electricity can be cut off. Similarly, when we keep receiving gifts from nature but do not reciprocate as per the universal system mentioned above, we are eventually deprived of the gifts.

But what should we do? Which yajnas should we perform? Do we have qualified people to perform them? Well, in the present age, yajnas are not practical due to the prohibitive costs of the required oblations as well as due to non-availability of competent priests to precisely chant the intricate mantras. Therefore, the Vedic texts recommend a method more pragmatic than fire sacrifices: sankirtan yajna, the devotional chanting of the Lord's holy names:

Hare Krishna Hare Krishna Krishna Krishna Hare Hare

Hare Rama Hare Rama Rama Rama Hare Hare

If we can simply engage in this one yajna, we shall be fulfilling our obligation to the Lord and no one will never face a shortage of any resources.

And this yajna does not cost anything or involve any complex mantras.

So yajnas are not a waste of money, but rather a duty, an act of gratitude and an obligation that we must fulfil to receive nature's gifts supplied by the demigods in charge of various necessities of life, as per the system designed by the Supreme Lord Krishna.

Q. 46

Can spirituality free one from stress and fear?

Yes, it can.

Kieth Ward, in his book *Is Religion Dangerous?*, writes:

'People who have a strong spiritual foundation tend to be mentally stronger, less prone to depression, hypertension and less vulnerable to criminal tendencies.'

Suppose you are walking on a lonely street, late at night. Suddenly you see a hefty, suspicious-looking person charging towards you. Just as fear starts creeping up your spine, you notice an armed policeman standing on guard nearby. Immediately your fear disappears.

Fear and anxiety come when we feel things are beyond our control. But spirituality teaches us that they might be beyond our control, but never beyond God's control. This gives us hope, and as long as we have hope, we survive.

In fact, the most prominent scriptures—the Bhagavad Gita and Srimad Bhagavatam—have manifested in times of acute distress.

Arjuna, a great warrior, was facing a dilemma, which led to his refusing to do his duty, and he was thus torn apart. In such a situation, he took shelter in Lord Krishna as his Guru, thus teaching us a very pertinent lesson in spirituality as to what to do when things go wrong. He then heard the Gita from Lord Krishna and emerged from his confusion inspired and ready to perform his sacred duty.

As in the above story, financial, familial, social, educational, professional or physical problems may come upon us at any moment, no matter who we are. These problems—even their very thought—trigger fear within us. But if we are able to see the Lord always by our side, ready to protect us whenever required, then our fears will subside. The Bhagavad Gita (5.29) describes that the Lord is always present in our hearts, but we need to refine our devotional vision to perceive his presence there. Two quick and effective ways to feel God's protective presence are: praying to Him and chanting His holy names.

Stress, fear and anxiety are conditions of the uncontrolled mind, and our Vedic wisdom suggests the best remedy: mantra meditation. It is interesting that the word mantra means '*manas trayate iti mantra*'—that which liberates the 'mind' or 'mann'. When we chant the mahamantra,

Hare Krishna Hare Krishna Krishna Krishna Hare Hare
Hare Rama Hare Rama Rama Rama Hare Hare

and simultaneously hear and concentrate on the sound of the mantra, it gradually calms the mind, thus greatly reducing our stress levels.

Another way to overcome fear is by illuminating ourselves with spiritual wisdom. When we enter a dark room, we imagine various dangers within it and feel fearful. But when we turn on the light, we see our fears to be baseless. Ignorance is darkness and knowledge is light. When we are spiritually uninformed, life is like a dark room for us, and so we often imagine things going wrong in the future and make ourselves fearful. When we turn on the light of divine wisdom in our own hearts, we understand the reality of life and why things are happening in a specific manner and how to respond to them. Thus illuminated, we learn to have realistic expectations, thereby reducing our stress levels.

Q. 47

How is a holy place different from any other place?

Holy places such as Vrindavan, Dwarka, Mathura, Jagannath Puri, Tirupati and many others are considered spiritual and different from others because they exist not just on the physical plane like other places, but also as a parallel reality on a higher-dimensional spiritual plane.

What makes a place holy is the presence of the Lord and holy people.

Wherever the Lord steps into and performs His pastimes and wherever His holy devotees are absorbed in His devotional service, is a holy place. The Lord has made His presence felt at such places. Holy people perform their devotional activities with love and dedication, creating even higher levels of spiritual purity and a powerful vibe all around. Thus, these places become surcharged with spiritual energy capable of even neutralizing our sinful karmas, the root cause of all our sufferings. When we are at these places, we tend to absorb the same energy and thus experience a great spiritual transformation and advancement, which would otherwise take many years to achieve in an ordinary place.

But all this is not mechanical. The powerful energy is all around, but to absorb it, we need an absorbing agent, which is our devotional practice of chanting the Lord's holy names and hearing His glories from scriptures such as the Bhagavad Gita and Srimad Bhagavatam. Many people visit holy places like tourists with the spirit of enjoyment and are unable to access the grace that is available there. But those who go to make spiritual advancement and acquire spiritual merits are blessed accordingly.

Visiting holy places is a very important part of Indian culture. The whole world is turning to India for spirituality and understanding their spiritual significance; lakhs of people from all over the world visit holy places in India every year.

Q. 48

What is the significance of Diwali?

With the passage of time, most of us have forgotten the reasons and the spirit behind the countless sacred occasions and rituals that our country boasts of celebrating every year. To carry on with something, we need two things: encouragement and enlightenment.

When there is only encouragement without enlightenment and vice versa, things don't last.

Many of us celebrate Diwali without knowing the reason behind it. Or even if we know a little about it, we are not conscious of the spirit. Most of us simply use it as an occasion to burst crackers, distribute sweets, buy new things and worship Goddess Laxmi for wealth. Hardly anyone remembers the real reason behind the celebration. And worst till, some people use this occasion to simply further their spirit of enjoyment through Diwali parties, playing cards etc. One simply wonders how are these activities related to Diwali or Lord Rama?

Selfishness is so deep rooted that we do not mind using (rather abusing) such holy days also to suit our own motives.

These are the days filled with immense grace and we should leave everything else and simply immerse ourselves in the remembrance of the Lord to access that divine grace. Unfortunately, over a period of time, the essence has been lost.

Diwali is one of the most popular festivals in the Indian calendar. The anniversaries of many auspicious historical events like the birth of Goddess Laxmi and Dhanvantari (god of Ayurveda) add value to this ancient festival.

This is the very day the jubilant citizens of Ayodhya welcomed Lord Rama back to their city after His exile. The Ramayana describes how when Lord Rama was exiled due to a conspiracy of Manthara and Kaikeyi, Ayodhya became a ghost city. All its citizens were plunged into an ocean of separation and sorrow for fourteen agonizing years. When Lord Rama finally returned, their hearts' innermost longing was at last fulfilled. They spontaneously celebrated this joyful reunion of divine love by illuminating their houses with lamps. There were lines (*avali*) of lamps (*deep*). Thus the name 'Deepavali'.

Apart from being a historical reality, this event also has immense relevance to our lives. Ayodhya is like our heart and Lord Rama is the Lord of our heart, the supreme object of love and devotion for all of us. Due to unfortunate misconceptions, we too have exiled the Lord from our heart. Just as Ayodhya became a ghost town when Lord Rama departed, our heart too has become infested with ghostly feelings like anxiety, boredom, loneliness, depression, stress, prejudice, envy, anger and hatred. And, just like the citizens of Ayodhya, our lives too have become filled with emptiness and lamentation.

But there is one important difference between us and the citizens of Ayodhya. They clearly knew that their grief was due to the absence of and separation from the Lord, whereas we do not know or are often slow to recognize this root cause of our miseries. We try to hide and forget the existential emptiness of our life by accelerating its pace in pursuit of mundane goals—wealth, enjoyment, entertainment, fame, power and position. But these illusory substitutes for our eternal connection with God can offer only flickering titillation, not lasting fulfilment. Consequently, despite the frenzied pace and the jazzy gadgets that are the pride of our lives, we remain largely unfulfilled and disappointed.

Historically, the import of Diwali is not the lighting of lamps, but the return of Lord Rama to Ayodhya. So our celebration of Diwali will remain incomplete if we continue to restrict ourselves to lighting lamps. Then how can we welcome the Lord back into our hearts and experience the essence of Diwali?

By chanting His holy names, worshiping His holy deity, remembering His example and applying His instructions in our daily life, and most importantly, sharing the same with others. Therefore, while lighting the earthen lamps this Diwali, let us also light our hearts with divine wisdom and love.

Q. 49

Is forgiveness possible, especially towards someone who repeatedly hurts us?

When someone hurts us, forgiving that person is our best response. But often our indignant emotions make us overlook the subtle but vital line that differentiates forgiving a person from trusting a person: forgiveness is for the past; trust is for the future. We are urged to immediately forgive, but not immediately trust the wrongdoer. Let's explore this difference.

Whatever wrongs a person has done in the past can't be changed; as long as we resent the past, we stay stuck in it. Consequently, our thoughts, words, actions and even lives may become resentment-driven, causing us to either clam up or blow up. When we clam up, we drive our anger deep within, thereby unnecessarily inflicting ugly scars on our psyches that may distort our personality. When we blow up, we drive our anger outward not just to the wrongdoer, but to whoever crosses our path at the time of blowing up, thereby hurting our reputation as well as an innocent person. Thus, both resentment-driven responses—clamming up or blowing up—are counterproductive.

Therefore, the best response is that which frees us from resentment—and forgiveness alone can do that. Forgiveness is necessary to move on. When we forgive a person, we accept the reality that the other person, being a fallible human, is imperfect—as are we. We too may err tomorrow and be in need of forgiveness. In fact, the logic of karma suggests that we may have hurt someone in the past, just as someone has hurt us now. We then see the wrongdoer not as the cause, but as the vehicle of our suffering, which originated in our own past insensitivity. Understanding this philosophically informed vision, we should not become angry with 'the instruments of our karma'. Even if our indignant feelings make the logic of karma difficult to digest, forgiveness retains its potential to free us from resentment.

Forgiving a person certainly doesn't mean that we let the other person continue the hurtful behaviour. We must gently but firmly draw a line and let the person know that they cannot cross it.

Once, a snake became a devotee by the instruction of the great devotee Narada Muni. Narada Muni instructed the snake to become non-violent and to no longer bite anyone.

Unfortunately, people took advantage of this non-violence on the part of the snake, especially the children, who began to throw stones at him.

He did not bite anyone, however, because his spiritual master had instructed him not to.

After a while, when the snake met Narada again, he complained, 'I have given up the bad habit of biting innocent living entities, but they are mistreating me by throwing stones at me.'

Upon hearing this, Narada Muni instructed him, 'Don't bite, but do not forget to expand your hood as if you are going to bite. Then they will go away.'

What we allow is what will continue. We need to find that balanced course of action that allows both us and the other person to grow.

To summarize, forgiveness involves our cultivating virtue independent of the other person, whereas trust is our reciprocation conditional to that person's cultivating virtue. By understanding the difference between the two, we can transform unfortunate episodes in our relationships into growth opportunities at least for ourselves—and possibly even for the other person.

Q. 50

Why does the Bhagavad Gita recommend working with detachment?

The Bhagavad Gita recommends cultivating a reasonable amount of detachment. Someone might find this disheartening or discouraging, but it is not. We must not forget it is the Supreme Lord, the greatest well-wisher of everyone, who has spoken the words in the Bhagavad Gita. There is a deeper reason behind why we should cultivate detachment.

1. **To save us from anxiety:** All of us work hard towards happiness and success, but the reality is that the results come based on our past karma or destiny. Sometimes the results might not be in our favour, and if we are attached to them, then we tend to become depressed. That is why the Bhagavad Gita tells us to be attached to doing our duty the best way we can, but not to be attached to the results, so we can avoid unnecessary mental trauma. It simply means that we should focus on what is within our control and not worry about what is beyond.

2. **To help us advance towards the ultimate goal:**
   The Bhagavad Gita speaks from the absolute eternal perspective. We are all spiritual beings, but at the moment, we are disconnected from Him due to being enamoured by our personal desires in terms of 'I, me and mine'. We behave selfishly, only concerned with our own happiness. However, we do not know where real happiness lies. Human life is meant for cultivating attachment to the spiritual, and to achieve this, detachment from matter is necessary. As long as we remain attached to matter, our liberation is impossible, and we will have to keep returning to the material world to undergo the same miseries again and again. Obsession with the short-term material results of work deprives us of the long-term spiritual results.

We can have immediate goals, no doubt, but let us not forget the ultimate goal.

How do we practice detachment?

At our stage, if we try to detach ourselves, we might end up becoming insensitive to others. To avoid this, the goal of detachment must be understood.

The goal of detachment is attachment to God.

For example, why does a doctor tell a patient to stop eating certain things? Because the person has been eating the wrong things. But is stopping his eating the goal of prohibition? Not at all! The goal is to restore his health, i.e., by cultivating healthy eating habits.

The natural health of living entities depends on how engaged we are in the devotional service of the Lord. Since we are wrongly engaged, the path of gradual detachment from our material engagement is recommended, so we can come back to our natural state. But if someone is already sincerely and seriously connected to the Lord through His service, He does not need to detach himself because the goal of detachment—attachment to God—has already been reached.

In fact, we can say that the Bhagavad Gita recommends the path of attachment, not detachment and that is why it is also known as 'yoga shastra'. 'Yoga' means to link or 'join' with the supreme. The Bhagavad Gita recommends the path of relinking with the supreme, without giving up anything, through karma, jnana, dhyana and ultimately bhakti, the supreme among all paths.

Thus, the Bhagavad Gita doesn't demotivate us by teaching us to neglect or reject the worldly results of our work, but it urges us not to get stuck in them and keep the higher goal in mind.

Q. 51

Why do natural calamities occur?

Natural calamities are a display of an awesome power that is greater than the human. They jolt us out of our complacent routines and impel us to think: Why do such natural disasters occur? How should we respond to them? Can we do anything to prevent their recurrence?

According to the great spiritual traditions of the world, we are answerable to God for all our actions. The Vedic texts of ancient India give the most coherent understanding of this system of cosmic accountability. Known as the law of karma, this universal, infallible law of action-reaction gives all of us our due pleasures and pains according to our actions, whether right or wrong. The Vedic texts therefore contain prescriptions and proscriptions to guide us in our actions. Anyone who violates these injunctions has only himself to blame for the consequences.

The Vedic scriptures explain that karmic punishment comes upon humanity in the form of three types of miseries called the '*tri-vidha tapa*' as given below:

1. Miseries caused by our own bodies and minds (*adhyatmika-klesha*), for example, fever, indigestion, stress, depression
2. Miseries caused by other living beings (*adhibhautika-klesha*), for example, mosquitoes, competitors, superiors, relatives
3. Miseries caused by higher natural powers (*adhidaivika-klesha*), for example, extreme heat or cold, floods, storms

Therefore, for the intelligent, the reality of karma is not difficult to see. We cannot break the law; we can only break ourselves against the law. A sceptic who jumps from the top of a hundred-storey building can imagine that there is no law of gravity—but only till he hits the ground. Similarly, we can go on with our godless sinful ways, imagining that there are no karmic laws, but only till the karmic reactions hit us as tsunamis or terrorism or wars or ecological disasters.

If we want to minimize the casualties due to natural calamities, better detection techniques alone will not suffice. Even if we detect a calamity in time and save ourselves from it, our karma will still give us our due suffering in some other way. Unlike the human penal system, karma is a flawless system of justice. By science or some other material means, we may alter how, when and where our karmic reactions come upon us, but we will never be able to escape them. Therefore, if we want to be saved from suffering, we have to scrupulously avoid bad karma. Furthermore, we can protect ourselves from our past misdeeds by reharmonizing ourselves with God. This can be easily and effectively done by adopting the non-sectarian, universal meditation on the holy names of God, especially the mahamantra:

> Hare Krishna Hare Krishna Krishna Krishna Hare Hare
> Hare Rama Hare Rama Rama Rama Hare Hare

When a criminal becomes law-abiding, the severity of punishment is often reduced. This principle is just as true in cosmic justice, for God is our benevolent Father. Even in this life and in this world, by harmonizing with God, we can be much more peaceful and joyful than by defying God.

And if we wish to truly help our fellow citizens on this planet, humanitarian aid will not be enough. We have to offer spiritual aid by giving the enlightenment and empowerment that comes from God consciousness. That alone will equip them to protect themselves from both bad karma and its reactions.

Q. 52

Why do we not get action-reaction (karma) in the same life?

Somebody may ask, 'Why should I suffer now for my actions in a previous life? Why so much delay?'

Different seeds fructify after different time durations. Grains harvest after two or three months, some fruit seeds produce fruits after twenty years and some seeds may take a hundred years to fructify. Every action that we perform is like a seed sown. The seed will fructify, and we cannot escape the result. One may say, 'I don't like this fruit, I don't want it.' But one will be forced to eat the fruit, even if it is thorny. The reactions will come, but different types of karma seeds (actions) have different time durations after which they fructify.

Why do different actions give reactions after different time durations? To understand this, let's probe deeper into the mechanism of karma, as is illustrated through an incident from the Mahabharata.

After the bloody Kurukshetra war, Dhritrarashtra asked Lord Krishna, 'I had a hundred sons and all of them were killed in the war. Why?' Lord replied, 'Fifty lifetimes ago, you were a hunter. While hunting, you tried to shoot a male bird, but it flew away. In anger, you ruthlessly slaughtered the hundred baby birds that were in its nest. The father-bird had to watch in helpless agony. Because you caused that father-bird the pain of seeing the death of his hundred sons, you too had to bear the pain of your hundred sons dying.'

Dhritarashtra said, 'But why did I have to wait for fifty lifetimes?' Lord Krishna answered, 'You were accumulating punya (pious credits) during the last fifty lifetimes to beget a hundred sons because that requires a lot of punya. Then you got the reaction for the papa (sin) that you had committed fifty lifetimes ago.'

Lord Krishna says in the Bhagavad Gita (4.17), '*gahana karmano gatih*', the way in which action and reaction works is very complex. God knows best which reaction must be given at what time and in what condition. Therefore, some reactions may come in this lifetime, some in the next and some in a lifetime in the distant future.

There is a saying, 'The mills of God grind slowly, but they grind exceedingly fine.' So, every single action will be accounted for, sooner or later. Srimad Bhagavatam gives the example: if we have a cowshed with a thousand calves and if we leave a mother cow there, she will easily find her calf among those thousands. She has this mystical ability. Similarly, our karma will find us among the millions of people on this planet. There may be thousands of people travelling on the road, but only one of them meets with an accident. It is not by chance, it is by karma. Thus, the law of karma works exceedingly fine; it may be slow to act, but no one can escape it.

Q. 53

Why are the ignorant not excused by the law of karma?

Once, a person riding a bike came to a red signal and slowed down. Then he saw a buffalo walking confidently across the road without considering the signal. Seeing this, he also started to move, and immediately, the traffic policeman stopped him and fined him. He asked the policeman, 'You didn't fine the buffalo, so why are you fining me?' The policeman replied, 'Because you are a bigger buffalo!'

The buffalo does not have the intelligence to understand the law, but we human beings do. If we are driving, it is not the government's duty to educate us about the laws of the state. It is our duty to learn the state laws. Similarly, if we are living in this world taking in its air, water, sunlight and food, we need to follow the rules laid down by God.

If one stays at a hotel, eats, sleeps, watches TV and so on, then obviously one will have to pay for all the facilities provided by the hotel. If the bill is not paid, a few reminders will come. And if the bill is still not paid, severe punishment is sure to come. At that time, one can't simply respond with, 'I did not know I had to pay the bill for staying at the hotel'.

Similarly, it is not for material nature to teach us our duties. It is for us to learn the laws of karma. After jumping from the top of a ten-storey building and breaking his bones, a child cannot say, 'I didn't know that if I jumped from a ten-storey building, I would fall down and break my bones'. The law of gravity will not excuse him. Just as the law of gravity is impartial and inexorable, so is the law of karma.

And ignorance is not an excuse for sin; rather, ignorance is the consequence of sin. For example, when a person commits a crime, he is put in jail. In a standard jail, often there are reformers who counsel the prisoners in an attempt to turn them into good citizens. But if in the jail also, the prisoner attacks his co-prisoners, counsellors and guards, he will be taken from the normal prison cell and put in a dark dungeon where he will be given food from the window, and nobody will come to give him counsel. Why is that? Because he rejected the opportunity for counselling earlier, he has now been put in a place where he receives no counselling.

Likewise, if somebody is born in a social situation or in a cultural environment where they do not learn about the law of karma, then it is because they have, by their past actions, shown God that they are not interested in knowing about His laws. That is why they have been put in a place where they have no opportunity to get to know about God. The current Kali Yuga is actually such a dark age. The souls who are born in Kali Yuga are the ones who, in the previous ages of Satya, Treta and Dwapar, have shown by their actions that they don't care for the laws of God. This is why many of them are born in a situation where they don't learn about the laws of God.

However, God is not just a judge. He is also a loving Father and thus arranges circumstances such that at least once during our life we have the opportunity to think about what we are living for, and what the purpose of life is. During such a time, the curtains of ignorance fall away and a stream of enlightenment begins to come through. If at that time we seek guidance and wisdom, then God will guide us to a place where we will surely obtain it.

Q. 54

Why do natural calamities kill thousands of innocent people?

Let us consider a lesser-known incident that took place during the tsunami disaster that struck the Indian subcontinent a few years ago.

On the morning of that disaster, just before the tsunami struck, some scuba divers went diving in the ocean to look for jewels. When they went underwater, they suddenly felt a force pushing them upwards. They struggled to resist the force till it subsided. Then they went deeper under the water, did their exploration, returned to the surface of the ocean and swam back to the coastline—only to find that there was no coastline! While they were under the water, the tsunami had devastated everything. Just consider, the tsunami killed those who were on the land, but those who were under the water were unharmed! If these scuba divers had ventured into the ocean a little later or a little earlier, they would have been on the surface when the killer wave hit. But by their karma they were not supposed to die at that time, so although they were closest to the tsunami, they did not die.

Another even more amazing example: During an earthquake in Gujarat, there was a mother who had a small baby suckling at her breast. Suddenly, the earthquake struck, and a column of the roof fell on the mother. The mother died on the spot. Almost twenty-four hours later, when the rescue workers worked their way down through the debris, they found the mother dead and the infant moving his hands and legs holding on to his mother's breast. An infant is so tender that one small blow can prove fatal for him, yet there he was, safe amidst a quake that proved fatal for many healthy adults.

What we learn from incidents like these is that although natural calamities kill en masse, they don't kill blindly.

Mass karma involves a group of people who have done different kinds of bad karmas. The reaction of their karma is that they are all supposed to leave this world. Material nature gives that reaction to many people efficiently in one stroke through a calamity. For example, all such people may be brought together in one airplane and that airplane will crash. The person who is not supposed to die will not be on that flight, perhaps because his car broke down on the way to the airport and he missed that flight.

In this way, *karmana daiva netrena*—the law of karma acts under the divine supervision of the Lord. Even in a mass calamity, not one person is killed blindly; everyone receives the reactions of their own karma.

Q. 55

Why does the Bhagavad Gita call for violence?

Life is not black and white. Rather, it is different shades of grey. The scriptures such as the Bhagavad Gita talk about general principles of dharma, but the application of these principles must be understood from a proper guru. Depending on a particular time, place and circumstance, dharma might become adharma and vice versa. For example, the Puranas tell a story where a butcher was running after a cow with a sword in hand. The cow ran by a Brahman's cottage and hid in the bushes. The Brahman had never lied in his life. When the butcher came and asked him where the cow was, the Brahman, not willing to lie at any cost, unhesitatingly pointed to the bush where the cow was. The butcher went and killed the poor living being. As a result, the Brahman had to go to hell to suffer. So, although he was right in following dharma, he was ignorant of its proper application. Truthfulness is one of the greatest virtues and lying is a sin, but in this case the virtue resulted in the destruction of an innocent life. Thus, it became a sin.

Similarly, dharma says that violence is bad, but in certain cases, it might be necessary. The Bhagavad Gita is the manual for human life and is a book of practical choices. It does not propagate violence, but teaches that in certain circumstances, it is necessary to maintain peace. That is why we have the United Nations Peacekeeping Force. Does it not sound contradictory? Force and peace? Yet it is not. To maintain peace, sometimes force is necessary. Violence is one of the extreme options used by those who protect the law when they have to keep a check on unwanted elements exploiting the innocent. A policeman cannot watch a criminal harming others and do nothing about it. He cannot say violence is bad. In fact, to save hundreds of people, he must be willing to punish the wrongdoer. If he does not do so, he is neglecting his duty.

In the Mahabharata, Lord Krishna and the Pandavas had tried everything they could to avoid war with the Kauravas. In fact, there is one full *parva,* the Udyoga Parva, which only talks about the efforts made by the Pandavas to avoid the fratricidal war. When Lord Krishna went as a peace messenger to the Kauravas on behalf of the Pandavas, He even proposed that Duryodhana could give just five villages to the Pandavas in the name of peace, and continue as the ruler of the world. The Pandavas would be happy with that and live as Duryodhana's allies. With such strong support, no one would ever be able to challenge him. The war could thus have been avoided and countless lives could have been saved. But Duryodhana refused, saying he would not even give the Pandavas enough land to drive a pin through.

Eventually, when all efforts to maintain peace failed, war, as the last option, was inevitable.

Lord Krishna descends to protect the pious, destroy the demoniac and establish dharma. He could not allow the world to be ruled by demonic forces led by people like Duryodhana and Dushasan. This is why He encouraged Arjuna to pick up his weapons and fight the war because it was about protecting dharma, and Arjuna, being a Kshatriya, was duty-bound to do so as much as a policeman is duty-bound to protect the law. We cannot be stubborn and stick to one stance without taking into consideration the time, place and circumstances. Violence is bad but in some cases this could be the only practical option left, especially when it comes to protecting others' honour. The intention justifies the means as we learn from the episode mentioned below.

A true incident:

Once, an ISKCON devotee was speaking at a gathering about how in some cases, violence is necessary. One man in the audience became furious at this and went on to shout at the devotee about how non-violence is the only way in all circumstances. He was not willing to listen or understand what the devotee was trying to say. Finally, the devotee asked him one simple question, 'What if someone tries to abduct your wife in front of your eyes? Would you remain quiet and not do anything? Would you still be non-violent?' The man was stunned, and everyone was staring at him, waiting for his answer. The man, however, just to protect his ego said, 'Yes! I would not do anything.' And the rest, as they say, is history.

His wife, who was sitting next to him, stormed out of the room, furious at hearing her husband's answer.

Thus, we see that the Bhagavad Gita teaches what is practical. Violence is necessary sometimes, but only to protect the innocent and uphold justice. However, if anyone tries to engage in it indiscriminately, he must be punished.

Q. 56

Isn't being good and doing good to others enough? I live honestly and do not harm others. Why do I need God?'

The Bhagavad Gita talks about three types of karma: karma, *vikarma* and *akarma*.

1. **Karma:** Commonly known as good karma or punya. Good deeds like helping the needy with food, clothing, shelter, medicine, education and so on.
2. **Vikarma:** Sinful activities like meat-eating, intoxication, illicit affairs, gambling, cheating, lying, hurting others verbally or physically etc.
3. **Akarma:** Activities performed in relation to God, like chanting of His names, worship of His deity form, building His temple, hearing His glories and message from the scriptures, using our money and resources to expand His service and mission etc.

Good karma can lead to a sense of peace, elevation to heavenly planets, a resultant good birth, an abundance of comforts and facilities etc.

Vikarma results in reactions such as future distress, legal implications, chronic disease and lower birth devoid sometimes of even basic necessities.

Even a little investment of our time in God's service can save us from the greatest calamities as is evident from the real-life episode of a lady named Satnam Kaur from North India. Some preachers of the Sikh religion were travelling from city to city, sharing the message from their holy scripture, the Guru Granth Sahib. One of them noticed a particular lady who would sit right in front at every gathering, no matter which city they were giving the sermon in. He was curious and decided to find out the reason behind her enthusiasm and dedication.

After a sermon, he approached her and said, 'I have seen you in every satsang (religious gathering) wherever we are. Even if the next satsang is five hundred kilometres away, you are seen sitting there listening attentively. Is everything all right? Is there anything that is troubling you? Is your family bothering you?'

She replied, 'My name is Satnam Kaur. And no. My family is very loving and supportive in every possible way. But something happened in my life after which I decided not to miss even a single satsang.'

She continued, 'Throughout my life I have done so much good work—feeding the poor, distributing medicines, blankets etc. There is no limit to how many philanthropic activities I have been involved in. I loved to do that, but I had no interest in satsang or God. My family would urge me to attend a satsang, but I was not interested at all.

'Once, they forced me to sit at a satsang, but I got bored and left after twenty minutes. Then one day, I died. I could see myself being dragged by some ferocious people who were extremely scary. They had bound me up with ropes and were dragging me down a path in a desert. The ground was burning hot and the sun above was relentless. They were yelling at me.

I felt thirsty and asked for some water, but they said, "There is no water here." They kept dragging me until we reached a river and they told me to go drink from it. As I went closer, I was horrified as I saw it was filled with obnoxious substances. I stepped back in disgust, saying, "No! I cannot drink this." They said, "Drink? you have to swim and cross this river."'

Satnam Kaur continued, 'I was perspiring and trembling, not knowing what to do. But then suddenly a young girl, around sixteen years old, appeared from nowhere and said, "Do not worry. I will help you." She just picked me up and with her mystic powers, placed me on the other side. I thanked her profusely, but she replied, "No, no! You do not need to thank me. I am here to help as a result of the twenty minutes of satsang that you did."

'I was shocked and asked, "Twenty minutes of satsang? What about all the good work that I did?"

'She replied, "For that you will get the rewards on this planet itself. But what protects us in times of our greatest need is the time and energy spent in connecting with God."

'After this startling revelation, she disappeared, and I was taken in front of Yamraja, the universal judge who judges living entities as per their karma and gives appropriate rewards and punishment.

'As soon as he saw me, he said to his messengers, "Oh! Who have you brought? Not this Satnam Kaur, but her neighbour Satnam Kaur had to be brought to me." As he said this, I woke up and initially thought it was a dream. But then, I saw myself covered in white, and my relatives, who had gathered around me, were sobbing. And then I heard some people crying in our neighbour's house, which made me believe that it was all true and the other Satnam Kaur had passed away.

'That day, I decided that if twenty minutes of satsang could bring me back to life and that was all that mattered in the end, I would never miss a single satsang, no matter where it took place. That is why you see me everywhere.'

This story is a classic example of how credits acquired from our good karmas are not enough. Only our devotional karmas will rescue us. Thus, along with being *good,* we also need to be *godly.*

Q. 57

Why do people commit suicide?

The desire to commit suicide springs from the thought that dying is less painful than living. According to the WHO, around 700 thousand people commit suicide every year. This number is greater than the number of people killed in wars, terrorist attacks and murderous crimes combined. WHO calls this disturbing global trend 'a tragic social health problem'.

Where are we heading? This data shows that the number of people killing themselves is greater than the number of people being killed by others. Isn't this alarming? One murder and there is so much hue and cry. One war and the whole world starts talking about it. Yet, more people are killing themselves and no one seems to be paying attention.

What brings us to such a stage?

When we begin to define our entire life by just one failure or one setback.

However, spirituality can help us transcend this stage in a more dignified way by offering a broader perspective about life.

Our Vedic scriptures explain that life is not a hundred-metre sprint, but a thousand-kilometre marathon where sometimes we fall down. But that fall is not the end of the world. We can always make a choice to get up and start running the marathon all over again.

Similarly, one failure is not proof that our entire life is a failure. One bad day does not mean we have a bad life. We can always learn from what went wrong and move on. Using every situation as a learning experience can help us deal with sabotaging thoughts. As the saying goes, 'Sometimes we win, sometimes we learn'.

When things are out of our control, we think they can't be managed. But spirituality teaches us that our life is a multi-innings game, and while things may be beyond our control, there is somebody sitting up there who is in complete control, and this gives us hope. As long as there is hope, we survive. It is only when someone is without hope that they decide to end their existence as they see neither a future nor light at the end of the tunnel.

A fish out of water will always be restless no matter what we facilitate it with. The Bhagavad Gita explains that we are spiritual beings and therefore the spiritual environment is our natural environment. The more we stay connected to our natural environment, the less restless we shall be.

When people lack spiritual knowledge, they naturally live for worldly goals. Their sense of identity and self-worth comes from the pursuit and achievement of materialistic aims such as wealth, sensual pleasure, possessions and position. This narrow-minded definition of success in terms of material achievements lies at the root of suicidal thought. Why? Because people pursuing such goals will sooner or later be confronted with a situation where they will fail to gain. And similarly, those who possess these things will be faced with situations where they lose or fear to lose what they live for. In such situations, people lose their identity and purpose, and they begin to feel that life is not worth living. And destroying one's very existence appears to be the only escape.

For example, a student who considers getting top grades to be his life's only goal will feel euphoric on becoming a topper. But he is equally prone to be devastated if he fails. If he thinks his only priority in life is achieving high scores, he may well consider his life a disgraceful failure if he fails to do so and decide to end it.

Spiritual practices like chanting the Lord's holy names (Hare Krishna Hare Krishna Krishna Krishna Hare Hare, Hare Rama Hare Rama Rama Rama Hare Hare), hearing from or studying the scriptures such as the Bhagavad Gita and Ramayana, meditating on the Lord's beautiful form, and associating with saintly people can help us remain in a positive state of mind. This will save us from self-destructive strategies such as suicide.

Sociological research confirms that the more a person prays to God, visits a temple or reads spiritual books, the less likely he is to commit suicide. And the more he dumps the spiritual side of life, the more likely he is to have suicidal tendencies. Let us therefore strive to assimilate and disseminate spiritual wisdom and help people lead balanced, meaningful, peaceful and cheerful lives.

Q. 58

Is work worship?

If all work is worship, then isn't the ass, which works the hardest, the greatest worshipper?

'Work' generally deals with the mundane—earning money, managing domestic affairs and satisfying bodily demands. 'Worship', on the other hand, usually focuses on the divine—prayer, chanting and meditation. So work and worship belong to two distinct domains, the mundane and the divine respectively. Can the two be wedded together?

Yes, of course. That is the path that the Bhagavad Gita recommends: the path of Karma Yoga.

We are eternal spiritual beings, beloved children of the Supreme Lord. But at the moment, we are disconnected from Him. We keep performing our work or karma in this world, but most of the time, the fruit of our labour remains our only and ultimate goal. If we get it, we are satisfied. Even if we do not, we feel it is all right as long as we do our work, and we think this is what life is about. But simply working is not enough. If our work helps us reconnect with the Supreme

Lord, only then does it become worship or Karma Yoga. Else it simply remains karma, which will eventually lead to bondage in the laws of karma.

Lord Krishna, in the Bhagavad Gita (8.7) recommends how we must work in this world:

tasmat sarvesu kalesu
mam anusmara yudhya ca
mayy arpita-mano-buddhir
mam evaisyasy asamsayah

'Therefore, Arjuna, you should always think of Me
in the form of Krsna and at the same time carry out
your prescribed duty of fighting. With your activities
dedicated to Me and your mind and intelligence fixed on
Me, you will attain Me without doubt.'

Hence, while performing our duties, we must simultaneously fix our consciousness on the Supreme Lord, which will make our work a sacred task.

To achieve this, we need to follow a daily programme of spiritual practice or sadhana such as chanting God's holy names and studying the scriptures, ideally in the morning. Sadhana creates a foundation of divine consciousness by which we can spiritualize the work of the rest of the day. In the morning, our consciousness is like wet cement. Whatever impressions are made at this time will stay with us throughout the day. It is important to begin our day on a divine note so that we can maintain divine consciousness through the day.

This will help us stay like a lotus in this world: being in this world, but not of this world, as even though a lotus leaf is surrounded by water, not even a single drop of water can stay on it. This way, our work becomes karma-free or truly a worship, an offering to the Lord.

We must have a life of balance. And a truly balanced life means not just advancing materially, but spiritually as well, which is the ultimate goal of human life. Have material goals, but remember to harmonize them with spiritual goals.

Q. 59

Is seeing believing? In the present scientific age, why should we believe in anything spiritual, especially in a God that cannot be seen?

To answer this, let us begin with an interesting story:

An atheistic professor of philosophy speaks to his class on the problem science has with God, the Almighty.

He asks one of his new students to stand and questions:

Professor: So, you believe in God?

Student: Absolutely, sir.

Professor: Science says you have five senses you use to identify and observe the world around you. Tell me, son, have you ever seen God?

Student: No, sir.

Professor: Tell us if you have ever heard your God?

Student: No, sir.

Professor: Have you ever felt your God, tasted your God, smelt your God? Have you ever had any sensory perception of God for that matter?

Student: No, sir. I'm afraid I haven't.

Professor: Yet you still believe in Him?

Student: Yes.

Professor: According to empirical, testable, demonstrable protocol, science says your God doesn't exist.

The student had no answer. He remained quiet for some time, but then finally spoke.

Student: Is there anyone in the class who has ever seen the professor's brain?

(*The class breaks out into laughter.*)

Student: Is there anyone here who has ever heard the professor's brain, felt it, touched or smelt it? No one appears to have done so. So, according to the established rules of empirical, testable, demonstrable protocol, science says that you have no brain, sir.

With all due respect, sir, how do we then trust your lectures?

(*The room is silent. The professor stares at the student, his expression unfathomable.*)

So, are we the centre of the universe? Are we perfect? Just because we cannot see something, does that mean it does not exist? So many people live in the city we live in. Have we seen them all? Have we seen all the places in the city or our country or the world for that matter? The obvious answer would be 'No'. But does our not having seen them defy their existence? Never! We must follow a process and go see them. We must make an effort!

There are so many things that we see, but do not believe.

For example, if we see our face in a concave mirror, it looks weird and deformed. But is it really like that?

When we put a rod inside a glass of water, it appears to be bent. But is it actually bent?

The earth and the sky appear to meet at the horizon. But do they actually meet?

Similarly, there are so many things that we are not able to see, but still believe in.

For example, oxygen, gravity, microorganisms and radio waves.

This proves that we have limitations. In fact, the Vedic scriptures explain that all humans are born with four defects. They are:

1. Imperfect senses (*karanapatava*)
2. Illusion (*bhram*)
3. The fallacy of committing mistakes (*pramada*)
4. The propensity to cheat (*vipralipsa*)

Among the imperfect senses, let us just consider the eyes, since the question concerns seeing.

Human eyes are only capable of seeing electromagnetic waves in the range of 390 to 700 millimicrons. Anything outside this thin band is not visible to us. There are many other wavelengths such as X-rays, radio waves etc. that are not visible to us. Even within the visible range, our eyes cannot see clearly if the light is too bright or too dim, if the object is too far or too close.

Our eyes do not have the capacity to see all material things properly, so how can they see something spiritual?

The first part of knowledge is humility. Humility to accept that we are not perfect, and we need guidance. As soon as we have this consciousness, truths will begin to reveal themselves to us.

Even though we cannot see God directly, His presence can be felt and seen through so many wonderful things in nature: seasons change cyclically, the sun rises and sets, the planets move in a perfect order, wonderful laws are in action such as the law of gravity, a variety of living beings exist, etc. Everything takes place systematically. If there is creation, there must be a creator. If there are laws, there must be a lawmaker. If there is order and design within the universe, there must be an intelligent designer.

Suppose we enter an office building and see everything is haywire—people look confused, some are shouting, some are fighting, things are scattered here and there. We would immediately ask, 'Is there no one in charge here?' However, if we see everything happening systematically and in perfect order, we conclude, 'There is some powerful, intelligent person behind this.'

Seeing so many wonderful phenomena taking place in the creation we live in, we can safely deduce that there must be a powerful person with a powerful brain behind it who is managing everything. And He is God.

When we see a wonderful pearl necklace, we glorify it for its beauty. But what is holding the pearls together, the thread, is not seen. And if the thread is broken, the pearls will scatter and the necklace will no longer exist. Similarly, this beautiful creation is like a beautiful necklace, and it is God who is holding it together. The presence of the unseen can be proven by the seen. He Himself says in the Bhagavad Gita (7.7):

mattah parataram nanyat
kinchid asti dhananjaya
mayi sarvam idam protam
sutre mani-gana iva

'O conqueror of wealth [Arjuna], there is no Truth superior to Me. Everything rests upon Me, as pearls are strung on a thread.'

'Seeing is believing' is an outdated belief that has long been rejected by science in its onward march. Scientists also follow the process of experimentation to verify what they come across before giving their conclusion. Then why should this principle (Seeing is believing) be allowed to block us on our onward spiritual march?

To see a microorganism, we need a microscope. To see a distant object, we need a telescope. We cannot interchange the apparatus. Similarly, to see God, we need a different method and apparatus. Material vision is not enough. But if we carefully observe and analyse the world around us, we will be forced to believe in the existence of the supreme being, God.

Ralph Waldo Emerson puts this conclusion well: 'All that I have seen teaches me to trust the Creator for all that I have not seen.'

Q. 60

Can we be spiritual, but not religious?

Yes, if by 'spiritual' we imply open-mindedness and by 'religion' close-mindedness. No, if by 'spiritual' we refer to a state of consciousness and by 'religious' a process to achieve that state of consciousness.

The intention to be 'spiritual-but not-religious' is laudable, but its application is questionable. Usually, the intention is that we should be broad-minded, not narrow-minded. That intention is fine, but is the underlying implication true? Is it true that spirituality makes us broad-minded and religion makes us narrow-minded?

These two terms 'spiritual' and 'religious' have so many connotations that without specifying their meaning, we cannot have a productive discussion. Let's focus on what these words normally refer to in the 'spiritual-not-religious' usage: 'spiritual' usually touches upon the experience of the higher, deeper aspects of life, whereas 'religious' refers to the adherence to certain beliefs and rituals given in a specific tradition. The implication is that spiritualists are open-minded because they are open to higher experience, whatever be the way they get that experience. But religionists are close-minded because they stick only to the way given in their own religion and deride the ways given in other religions.

The Vedic wisdom-tradition points to an intriguing relationship between spirituality and religion. It explains that spirituality is meant to help us reconnect with our higher self (which is spiritual) and ultimately reconnect with God. This is done through a harmonious combination of philosophy and religion, which constitute the two rails on which spirituality runs. The philosophy aspect of spirituality involves the study and understanding of scriptures and the religion aspect involves the following of certain rules and regulations that help us realize and experience higher spiritual truths.

These two aspects of spirituality are strikingly similar to the two aspects of modern science: the theoretical and the experimental. Science's theoretical aspect involves formulating hypotheses to explain the observable phenomena within the universe. It is similar to the philosophy aspect of spirituality. Science's experimental aspect involves the following of certain rules to verify the hypotheses. It is similar to the religion aspect of spirituality. Without the application of what we hear or in other words, without following a process with certain rules and regulations under someone's guidance, it will be impossible to gain an experience of spirituality.

Just as science requires some kind of experimentation to be complete, spirituality requires some kind of religion to be complete. That is, spiritualists who want higher experiences need a process by which to get those experiences consistently.

And that process would be their religion. So, to be spiritual, one would have to be religious in some way or the other.

Many people take up reading spiritual books as a hobby, accepting themselves as uncommitted spiritual explorers or as academic scholars. Sometimes they might even attend spiritual discourses. But they don't practice any religion. Consequently, they rarely realize, or experience as a reality, the subject that they are reading. By their refusal to practice any religion, they deprive themselves of such realization. So, their thoughts and talks about spirituality remain airy mental speculations without a tangible connection to spiritual reality.

Before making this statement, 'I am spiritual, but not religious', we must look into our hearts and see that we are not fooling ourselves. Sometimes people use this statement because they simply want the label of being spiritual so they can say, 'I also go for spiritual discourses!' Or sometimes they use this tagline as an excuse to justify their non-beliefs and indifference to the path. But they wouldn't want to listen to or discuss God. Spirituality minus God is simply a pretence and a waste of time. We are only following ourselves if our spirituality is not leading us towards God. Better than this would be to be a diehard atheist because then at least we know who we are and are not confused about our own identity.

If those wanting to be 'spiritual-not-religious' deliberately avoid religion in terms of not adopting any religious practices, then they will remain mental speculators. They may occasionally have experiences that they consider 'spiritual', but they will gain no lasting transformation of heart and so will not find enduring fulfilment in life.

Q. 61

Which is the best, easiest and most practical form of spiritual practice in today's day and age?

Anything that we do, if it is supported by the scriptures, will have a lasting impact as the scriptures are the real manuals for human life.

When we are sick with a cold, there are several medicines available in the market to cure the same. But do we just go to the chemist and pick up whichever medicine we like? No! We must refer to the prescription of a doctor who will recommend a specific medicine after seeing the symptoms. Similarly, when it comes to spiritual practice, we must refer to the supreme doctor God Himself who, in the scriptures, has recommended the best form of spiritual practice for this particular yuga (Kali Yuga) we are living in, i.e., the chanting of His holy names. Srimad Bhagavatam (12.3.52) says:

krite yad dhyayato vishum
tretayam yajato makhaih

dvapare paricaryayam
kalau tad dhari-kirtanat

'Whatever result was obtained in Satya-yuga by
meditation on Vishnu, in Treta-yuga by performing
sacrifices, and in Dvapara-yuga by serving the Lord's
lotus feet can be obtained in Kali-yuga simply by
chanting the names of Lord Hari.'

But the Lord has many names. Which ones are to be chanted?

Let us refer to a discussion from the Kali-Santaran
Upanishad (1-6, 8-9):

1. 'Hari Om! After travelling all over the world, Shrila
   Narada Muni approached Lord Brahma (his own father
   and guru) during the time when Dvapara-yuga was about
   to end. He asked him, "O Lord! How will all the living
   entities be able to deliver themselves from the most
   degraded age of Kali which is about to begin?"
2. Lord Brahma replied, "You have asked the most relevant
   question for the benefit of humanity. I will tell you now
   the most concealed secret of the Vedic literatures, with
   the help of which everyone can easily cross this most
   dangerous age of Kali.
3. "Simply by chanting the transcendental names of the
   original enjoyer and the Supreme Personality of Godhead,
   Lord Narayana, all the sins will be cleansed in Kali-yuga."
4. Narada Muni again asked, "Which are those specific
   names of the Lord which are most effective in Kali-yuga?"

sa hovaca hiranyagarbah
hare krishna hare krishna, krishna krishna hare hare.
hare rama hare rama, rama rama hare hare; [5]
iti shodashakam namnam, kali-kalmasha-nashanam;
natah parataropayah, sarva-vedeshu drishyate. [6]

5-6. Lord Brahma replied, "The sixteen words—Hare
Krishna, Hare Krishna, Krishna
Krishna, Hare Hare; Hare Rama, Hare Rama, Rama
Rama, Hare Hare—are especially meant for completely
destroying all the contamination of Kali.
To save oneself from the contamination of Kali-yuga,
there is no alternative in all the Vedas except the
chanting of this sixteen-word mantra."

8. Shrila Narada again inquired, "What are the procedures
    and rules for chanting this mahamantra?"
9. Lord Brahma replied, "There are no rules and regulations
    to chant this mahamantra. It should be chanted always
    irrespective of whether one is in a pure or impure
    condition.

We can chant while sitting, walking, before taking bath
or after. But whenever we chant, we must try to hear it as
attentively as possibly to receive its benefits.'"

Thus, chanting the names of Lord Hari or Krishna is
the best form of spiritual practice as it is approved by the
scriptures and all the previous spiritual preceptors. Still, we

are free to try other things if we wish to, but they will not be as effective.

When we chant the Hare Krishna mahamantra and meditate on its sound, the mind becomes gradually calmer and cleansed of negativity. In fact, it is the most powerful weapon to control the mind. In addition, it builds an armour so no further negativity can enter the mind. While we chant, the mind will wander. As soon as we realize this, we must bring it back to the sound of the mantra and keep focusing on one mantra at a time to see the magic that manifests.

Q. 62

Was Arjuna's killing of Karna, when the latter was chariot-less, unfair and against the Kshatriya codes?

Not at all!

If we read the Mahabharata, we find that the word 'unfair' was synonymous with the Kauravas. Since the Pandavas were born, the Kaurava prince Duryodhana and his brothers had conspired every single day to eliminate them but were unsuccessful.

Before the war at Kurukshetra began, warriors from both sides had agreed upon certain codes to be followed by both sides. Dhrishtadyumna, the commander-in-chief of the Pandavas, had declared that their side would not break the war codes first, but if the Kauravas did so, then the Pandavas would not be obliged to stick to the same.

One of the codes was that a chariot-less warrior should not be attacked, but the Kauravas violated it first. On the thirteenth day of the war, six of their prominent warriors including Karna ganged up to kill the chariot-less young Abhimanyu. Karna, being a party to the violation, was paid back in kind.

On the fourteenth day of the war, when Arjuna was striving to fulfil his vow to kill Jayadratha by sunset, his horses got exhausted and needed rest and water. While Lord Krishna led the horses away, Arjuna had to dismount from his chariot. Even on seeing him chariot-less, the Kaurava forces did not stop attacking him. In fact, they attacked him with greater ferocity, hoping to kill him. Still Arjuna held them back with his expert archery while simultaneously using mystical weapons to arrange for shade and water for his horses. Arjuna, even though unfairly attacked, didn't complain—and thus, neither should Karna have.

Karna himself violated that specific code on the seventeenth day during his confrontation with Arjuna. When Karna sent an unstoppable mystical weapon at Arjuna's head, Lord Krishna forcefully pushed the chariot into the ground so that the arrow hit Arjuna's crown instead of his head. Arjuna's life was saved, but his chariot got stuck in the ground. While Lord Krishna jumped off the chariot to free it, Arjuna was disadvantaged with an immobile chariot. Karna still attacked him, and Arjuna didn't ask to be spared but fought back and defended himself.

One of the codes was to not attack the other side after the sun had set. Even this rule was broken when the Kauravas, foreseeing their imminent defeat, attacked the Pandavas in the dark. But the Pandavas, with the help of mighty Ghatotkach, resisted and neutralized the Kaurava forces.

So in the final confrontation, Karna's reminder of the Kshatriya code was hypocritical. When Karna tried to take the high moral ground, Lord Krishna exposed him by listing all the times when Karna had disregarded morality. Lord Krishna's fitting response silenced Karna, who hung his head in shame.

Krishna demonstrated the principle: *shatho shathyam*— with the cunning, one can be cunning—and asked Arjuna to shoot Karna. Karna could have fought from the ground itself, as Arjuna had on the fourteenth day, but he was focused instead on complaining about how it was unfair, and this blunder cost him his life.

The Pandavas simply followed the rules mutually agreed upon, and it was the Kauravas who, time and again, took to manipulating them.

Q. 63

Why did Bhima kill Duryodhana unfairly by hitting him below the waist during their final battle in the Mahabharata war?

Due to his mother Gandhari's blessing, Duryodhana's body was invincible. Thus, the fight between Duryodhana and Bhima was not a normal mace fight where both warriors were equally matched. It was an unfair match since Duryodhana was protected by his mother's benediction and could come to no harm no matter how expertly or forcefully Bhima hit him with his mace. Bhima, on the other hand, had no such protection.

How long could Bhima go on fighting in such circumstances, especially when Duryodhana was counter-attacking and wounding Bhima? Among the many of Duryodhana's blows that hit Bhima, two were so brutal that they would have instantaneously killed a lesser warrior. Though Bhima was badly injured by those devastating blows, he, with his superhuman fighting spirit, maintained a stoic face, showing no weaknesses. His plight was like that of a bowler carted for six sixes in two successive overs. Actually, Bhima's plight was a million times worse. Why? Because Duryodhana's blows were wounding not just Bhima's morale, but also his body. It is akin to the batsman's shots hitting the bowler, thus rendering him less and less capable of bowling, while still being expected to go on bowling till death.

Can we really blame the battered bowler if he takes the only way out of the carnage: bowl bodyline and get rid of the batsman, retired hurt? If we were being wounded like that, can we be sure that we too wouldn't do something similar?

In addition, we must know that destiny is supreme, due to which the following reasons contributed to what transpired in this battle:

1. Maitreya Rishi had cursed Duryodhana that he would die due to the breaking of his thighs and Bhima was simply an instrument for fulfilling the sage's curse.
2. Bhima had vowed to break Duryodhana's thighs for having obscenely exposed those thighs to publicly humiliate Draupadi—and he had to do whatever it took to fulfil his vow.

As Lord Krishna also later said, there was no other way Bhima could have won, so he had to take the only way available. Duryodhana had to die, and this was the way he was destined to die.

Q. 64

If God created everything, who created God?

The very word 'God' refers to 'the source of everything and everyone'. So how can someone who is the source of all, have a source? Vedic literature provides us with the definition of God: '*sarva karana karanam*'. ('He is the cause of all causes.') This definition implies that, while tracing the origin of all the things around us, the point where we stop is God. If God were to have an origin, then that origin would be God Himself. Because even according to pure logic, the source of everything cannot have a source. So this question is itself illogical as it originates in an illogical understanding of the term, God.

Once a person read a novel for the first time in his life. On coming to know that the novel was written by an author, he asked, 'Where is the author in the novel?' The above question is similar. The answer obviously is that the author is not in the novel; he created the timeline, the storyline and the characters in the novel, but he exists outside of it. Similarly, God created time, space and everything else, including all of us, but He himself exists outside the fabric of time and space. So everything that exists within time and space needs a beginning, a cause, but God, Who exists outside it, needs no cause, for He is the cause of time and space; He exists outside the chain of creator and created.

Q. 65

Who is a guru? How do we find him?

Anyone who is born as a human being must have a guru. Why? To achieve perfection in the goal of human life.

Out of all 8.4 million species of life, only the human form is especially given or blessed with the ability to put an end to the transmigration of the soul or the cycle of birth and death. It is especially meant to realize God. To help us achieve this, a guru is a must.

In any field, whether we want to become a doctor or an engineer or a sportsperson, we need the help of an expert in that field. We might address him as coach, guide, mentor etc. When it comes to spirituality, we address him as 'guru'.

But who is a real guru?

Is someone who is a good orator to be considered a guru?

Is someone who is charismatic a guru?

Can someone who is famous be termed as a guru?

Is someone who has a great following all over the world a guru?

The answer to all these questions is a big NO!

Unfortunately, this has become the standard now, and then people complain that they get cheated. We get cheated because we want to be cheated. If we hear from our scriptures, we won't get cheated.

The position of a guru is clearly defined in the ancient scriptures.

1. A guru is someone who connects us with God.

For example, the position of a chief financial officer is created in a company to deal with the finances. But if he does not carry out his duty, he will not be considered a chief financial officer. He will be fired.

Similarly, the position of guru has been created by God to lead us to Him. So the one who doesn't do so must be rejected as a guru. In fact, he must be dismissed as a cheater.

2. A guru must be a devotee of God.

We can only give what we have. If a guru himself lacks devotion and connection to God, how can he give it to others and thus perform his real duty?

A real guru is someone who knows God, is dedicated to the service of God and also engages his followers in the same.

In fact, unless the guru is a devotee of Lord Krishna, he cannot understand transcendental knowledge, and he cannot even dream of imparting it to others.

Often, we come across people who claim to be gurus, but they do not even know who God is. So how can they connect with Him? And how can they connect others with Him? They will say God is nature, God is love, God is formless or everyone is God. They offer such vague answers because they do not know anything, and thus they fool innocent people.

3. A Guru must be part of a disciplic line/succession (*guru shishya parampara*).

The Padma Puran describes four disciplic lines authorized by the Supreme Lord Krishna to distribute knowledge about Him. They are:

1) **Shri Sampradaya:** Originates from Goddess Laxmi
   Earthly Acharya or Spiritual Master: Shri Ramanujacharya
2) **Kumar Sampradaya:** Headed by the four sons of Lord Brahma (Sanak, Sanatan, Sanandan and Sanat Kumar)
   Earthly Acharya: Shri Nimbarkacharya
3) **Rudra Sampradaya:** Headed by Lord Shiva
   Earthly Acharya: Shri Vishnu Swami
   Pusti Marg started by Shri Vallabhacharya is also a part of Rudra Sampradaya.
4) **Brahma Sampradaya:** Headed by Lord Brahma
   Earthly Acharya: Shri Madhvacharya

Any guru must be connected to one of these four disciplic lines.

If we receive teachings from a person who is not from one of these lines (and it is absolutely our choice), we will not receive perfect teachings.

4. A real guru must be a Vaishnava.
The Padma Puran states:

> *sat-karma nipuno vipro mantra-tantra-visaradah*
> *avaisnavo guru na syad vaisnavah sva-paco guruh*

A Brahman may be an expert in mantras, rituals and the six kinds of brahminical work (performing and teaching sacrifice, studying and teaching scripture, giving and receiving charity), but if he is not a Vaishnava (a devotee of Lord Krishna or Vishnu), he cannot be a guru. On the other hand, a Vaishnava, even if born in a family of untouchables, may be a guru.

5. A real guru must have all his senses under control.
In the Upadeshamrita (1.1), Srila Rupa Goswami mentions:

> *vacho vegam manasah krodha vegam*
> *jihva-vegam udaropastha-vegam*
> *etan vegan yo vishaheta dhirah*
> *sarvam apimam prthivim sa shisyat*

'A sober person who can tolerate the urge to speak, the mind's demands, the actions of anger and the urges

of the tongue, belly and genitals is qualified to make
disciples all over the world.'

6. A real guru must always speak from and refer to the scriptures.

If a person does not quote *shashtra* (scriptures) to authenticate
or support what he says and simply keeps giving his own
opinion on things, then he is not a Guru, but like any other
common man who simply speaks what comes to his mind.

A Guru is a messenger of God and thus he must simply
repeat God's message, which is found in the scriptures.

Just like a Guru must test a disciple before accepting him,
an aspiring disciple or follower must test the Guru before
accepting or following him by putting him through the
litmus test of the above- mentioned points.

How do we come across a faithful Guru? Well! As soon
as we desire to know Him (God) or search for a Guru, the
Lord sitting in our heart as a super soul/Parmatma will make
an arrangement for us. His representative as a Guru will come
and stand in front of us or we shall be guided to him.

But what type of Guru that will enters our life will depend
upon the sincerity of our heart.

If our desire is 50 per cent sincere, then that kind of
person will enter our life to guide us, and if we are extremely
serious about reaching the ultimate goal of human life, to
know God, then that kind of a guru will be sent by the Lord.

So essentially, finding a real guru or him finding us
completely depends on our own desire.

Q. 66

Are the Gods of different religions different?

No, all religions are different ways to reach the same God. Misunderstanding of this one principle has led to wars in the name of religion.

Just like different colleges affiliated to the same university teach the same subject matter, different religions teach us about the same God, but in slightly different ways keeping in mind the intellectual calibre of their followers. Depending on time, place and circumstance, that God is referred to differently in different religions. For instance, the sun can be called Surya, Ravi, Bhaskar or Suraj. It can be called by different names in different languages. Similarly, the same being, the Absolute Truth—God—is referred to by different names in different religions.

Allah can refer to His all merciful, all kind aspects. Jehovah can refer to His all-powerful aspects, Lord Rama refers to His joyous aspects, Lord Krishna refers to His all-attractive aspects. If we carefully study the scriptures of the great religions—the Bible, the Quran, the Bhagavad Gita—

we find that similar attributes are described for God. For example, the Bible says, 'I am the alpha and omega of all things'.

Lord Krishna says in the Bhagavad Gita (10.20):

aham atma gudakesa
sarva-bhutasaya-sthitah
aham adis ca madhyam ca
bhutanam anta eva ca

'I am the Super soul, O Arjuna, seated in the hearts of all
living entities. I am the beginning, the middle and the
end of all beings.'

Similarly, the Quran talks about how Allah is the beginning, middle and end of all things. So, if we look beyond fanatic beliefs, just as we look beyond the names of the sun, we will see that although the names are different, the object is the same.

Everyone agrees there is only one God (the Supreme Being). There cannot be many Supremes. But then, people say, 'my God is better than your God' or 'my God is the only way'. This is due to ignorance and lack of maturity. Only if we recognize that we have one universal father can we live in universal brotherhood.

Q. 67

Why should we spend on temples when we can serve poor people or open hospitals?

We certainly can serve the poor or contribute to opening hospitals, but why do we have to put the two activities in competition with each other? Why should service to God be seen as a competitor to serving poor people or opening hospitals?

Amazingly, people display such an attitude only when it comes to temples, and not when it comes to other activities related to their personal enjoyment.

If we wish to save money and serve the poor, then why not try and save in other activities as well, such as watching a cricket match or a movie. If the money that is spent by people on watching movies was used to feed the poor, twenty generations of poor people would be fed. That is the revenue of the entertainment industry. Huge, isn't it?

There is so much food wasted at parties and weddings and so much spent on organizing these events, but we do not question them. Yet when it comes to serving God, our love for the poor suddenly awakens. Isn't this hypocrisy?

The point here is not that we should not spend on weddings, as they are a sacred affair. The point is that when we put forward such arguments, we must analyse our own life honestly to understand why we are saying such things. Is it out of a genuine love for the poor or some deep-rooted hatred towards God and His service?

The two types of activities being talked about above, service to God and service to humanity, are not comparable.

Devotion or service to God is one part of our life and social service is another part of our life. The two are two different types of activities. Both have their place in our lives. Just as we don't compare entertainment with social service, we shouldn't compare social services to devotional services. They all have their place in our lives and they all cannot be put in competition.

One is service at the level of the body while the other is service at the level of the soul. And as the Bhagavad Gita states, we are the eternal souls. This is our true identity. We are not the body. Thus, service at the level of the soul is real service and in fact, the most important service. And temples render this service. They offer food for starving souls.

Just as educational institutions serve society in a certain way and hospitals serve in a certain way, temples also serve in a specific way. They serve as hospitals for the sick mind and to remove the poverty of the heart, which is the root cause of external poverty.

Why are people poor? The poverty in this world is not because of a shortage of resources but due to mismanagement of resources. According to WHO statistics, dated 9 June 2021:

- Worldwide obesity has nearly tripled since 1975.
- In 2016, more than 1.9 billion adults, 18 years and older, were overweight. Of these over 690 million were obese.
- 39 per cent of adults aged 18 years and over were overweight in 2016, and 13 per cent were obese.
- Most of the world's population live in countries where overweight and obesity kills more people than underweight.
- 39 million children under the age of 5 were overweight or obese in 2020.
- Over 340 million children and adolescents aged 5-19 were overweight or obese in 2016.

The same report also says;

- Although 1.9 billion adults are overweight or obese, 462 million are underweight.

That means more people are suffering because of too much food than because of a lack of food. The amount of money that only Americans spend on losing weight is enough to feed all the hungry people in the world. Thus, the problem here is not of shortage, but of the uncontrolled mind and greed. This is where temples, through spirituality, play an important role. They provide an environment and a process to cleanse our hearts from all misgivings.

Without a spiritual foundation, much of social service, unfortunately, becomes like pouring water in a leaking tank.

One of America's prominent thinkers, Henry David Thoreau, said that one hacking at the root of the tree of evil is superior to a thousand hacking at the shoots of that tree. You can cut a thousand branches, but they will all grow back. But if you uproot the tree, it will not survive. So, if somebody is hungry, we give them food. If somebody is sick, we give them medicine—and while these are all good activities, the ailment will keep recurring. Spirituality goes to the root cause of the problem: Why is the person in need in the first place? The answer is his past karmas. Giving food or medicine will only solve the problem externally, but will not take care of a person's karmas. Only their connection to God will. So the greater welfare work is to raise people's consciousness to God consciousness. We must serve the poor by providing material help, but simultaneously, we must also try to give them a divine connection so their stock of karma can be destroyed and they won't have to face the same miseries again in the future.

As far as others in society are concerned, spirituality offered by temples can empower them to bring out their better side. It encourages them to become more self-controlled and charitable. This is like hacking at the root of the tree. It is the most sustainable solution.

So yes! We must serve the poor and serve God. Since this whole creation is like His body, His pleasure will ensure happiness all around. As Srimad Bhagavatam (4.31.14) states:

yatha taror mula-nishechanena
tripyanti tat-skandha-bhujopashakhah
pranopaharach cha yathendriyanam
tathaiva sarvarhanam achyutejya

'As pouring water on the root of a tree energizes the trunk, branches, twigs and everything else, and as supplying food to the stomach enlivens the senses and limbs of the body, simply worshiping the Supreme Personality of Godhead through devotional service automatically satisfies everyone who is a part of that Supreme Lord.'

Temples help to reinforce faith in the above principle.

Thus, serving God in temples is not separate from social service, but a more complete form of the same.

Q. 68

Are the scriptures valid?

To accept anything blindly is certainly bad. But to reject something blindly is worse.

If we do not have faith because we consider ourselves to be students of science, then we must remember that science also proves or disproves a theory only after proper experimentation and doesn't just dismiss it.

Scriptures have stood the test of time. For us, there are three ways to check their authenticity:

1. Manuals
2. Axiomatic truths
3. Astonishing predictions

1. **Manuals:** Whenever we buy a gadget, we get a manual along with it. The manual tells us which buttons to press to get specific things done. If the gadget works the way the manual tells us it will, then the manual must be true.

Similarly, if we do not have faith in the scriptures, we should not reject them. We can try applying the principles mentioned in them in our life and see if they work. If they don't, we can always give up. But if we look around us, we will find that practices such as meditation, yoga and kirtan are becoming increasingly popular all over the world for the benefits they offer, and these practices come from our scriptures. We can apply the same in our life and see for ourselves the impact that they have.

2. **Axiomatic truths:** An axiomatic truth is a truth that needs no verification.

There are many such truths mentioned in the Vedic scriptures that were earlier rejected, but have now been verified and embraced by science.

Some of them are:

- Cow dung is pure. No one could believe that the dung of an animal could be pure. The scriptures mention only cow dung to be pure and not the dung of any other animal. Sometimes we see that when a yajna is about to take place, the place is smeared with Cow dung and Cow dung cakes are even used for the ritual. The same is not true for any other living entity.
- The earth is round. Earlier everyone believed that it was flat.
- Plants have life (are living beings). It was only around the 1950s after Jagdish Chandra Bose proved this that everyone else started accepting this fact.

- Child within the womb. Sonography is a recent invention (around 1970) that shows us the growth of the child within a mother's womb. But Srimad Bhagavatam, the greatest scripture, compiled by Vyasadev around five thousand years ago, mentions the child within the womb in the third canto and that too in great detail.

3. **Astonishing predictions:** The Vedic scriptures also make accurate predictions of incarnations of great personalities who will appear in the future. Some of the personalities predicted to be reborn, along with the text in which they are mentioned, are given below:

- Buddha (Srimad Bhagavatam 1.3.24)
- Chanakya (Srimad Bhagavatam 12.1.11)
- Chaitanya Mahaprabhu (Mahabharata Ml 92.15, Srimad Bhagavatam 11.5.32)
- Chandragupta and Emperor Ashoka (Srimad Bhagavatam 12.1.12)
- Jesus and Mohammed (Bhavishya Purana, Atharva Veda, Kanda 20, Shukta 127, 1-3)

There are also vivid predictions about the degradations that will occur in Kali Yuga (the current age). Some of them are:

- Food will be sold publicly in marketplaces. (In the past, food was never sold; it was only given in charity. But nowadays, every third shop sells food items.)

- Might will be right. (In the past, a person was respected for his learning. But nowadays it is only wealth or brute force that commands respect.)
- A Brahman will be known simply by the thread he wears. (A real Brahman is one who possesses the qualities of a Brahman, such as peacefulness, self-control, austerity etc.)

If the scriptures are of mundane origin, then how is it possible for them to state profound truths that modern science has only recently started discovering?

How can scriptures make accurate predictions about future occurrences? The answer is obvious: the scriptures have come from one who is all knowing, who knows the past, present and future. In other words, the Vedas are the words of God and thus perfect.

Q. 69

Why was Ekalavya treated so unfairly?

Ekalavya belonged to the Nishadha dynasty, which was, by nature, violent. That was why they were made to live in the mountains and forests because had they lived in the midst of wider society, they would have acted according to their nature and disrupted its harmony. Vedic culture accommodates everyone, but at the same time it is not blind.

Drona's academy was like an elite group because it was meant for Kshatriyas who were from well-known and respectable families. Ekalavya's tribe had in the past acted inimically towards the Kurus. Since Drona was a priest of the Kuru dynasty, he chose not to allow Ekalavya to join the academy, which was justified.

Ekalavya, who wanted nothing more than to learn from Drona, then decided to make an effigy or an image of Drona. He would hide behind a tree when Drona would give archery lessons to his students and thus secretly learn. He would then practice after taking blessings from Drona's effigy. He was skilled and thus became an extraordinary archer.

After having learnt archery, he then naturally wanted to exhibit his skill. Once when he was practicing in the forest, Drona and Arjuna happened to be walking by the area and came upon a dog barking. Ekalavya heard the dog barking too and did not want to be disturbed. So he shot a set of arrows at it and sealed the mouth of the dog completely. When Arjuna and Drona saw this, they marvelled at the expert archery skill that could seal the mouth of a dog like that.

However, the dog was not a dangerous creature, and its barking was natural. To seal a dog's mouth just because it barked appeared to be an excessive thing to do.

As Drona stood observing the dog, Ekalavya came to him and offered his respects. He said, 'I am your student. I have learnt from you.' Drona recognized him and said, 'If you consider yourself to be my student, then you should give me guru dakshina.' Then, he asked Ekalavya for his thumb, which Ekalavya gave him. Certainly, Ekalavya's offering of his thumb is a remarkable act of devotion to his guru.

However, why did Drona ask for such a guru dakshina? Why did Drona want to ruin the career of a person who was in a sense, a self-made man, who had worked hard?

Because Drona viewed the situation from a long-term perspective. For a person to contribute constructively in their life, both competence and character are required. Competence without character is disastrous. For example, if an expert doctor who is supposed to save lives lacks character, he might end up taking lives.

Since Ekalavya belonged to a particular community, Drona had questions about whether or not his character was sound because our environment, family etc. build our character. He also had questions about whether Ekalavya would use his archery skills to benefit or harm society. And when he saw Ekalavya silencing a dog by using his archery skills, it confirmed to Drona that while Ekalavya was a skilled archer, he did not have the character to use his skills in a discerning or thoughtful way. Since he used them indiscriminately, he needed to be punished not like a criminal, but rather by curtailing his powers. Otherwise, he would harm others.

One way to curtail his power was by asking for his thumb. Drona's primary consideration for asking Ekalavya for his thumb was to avoid the abuse of his power of archery and not because he wanted Arjuna to be the best archer.

The Mahabharata tells us that eventually, Ekalava joined the ranks of the demoniac king Jarasandha, with whom Lord Krishna fought. Lord Krishna killed Ekalavya. Ekalavya choosing the side of a demoniac king like Jarasandha also confirms that he was not the sort of person who would use power to protect others. Power corrupts, and if it lies in the hands of the immoral it can be destructive for everyone.

Unfortunately, we live in a society where good people are rarely appreciated and the unscrupulous allowed to play their victim cards.

Ekalavya's one act of devotion to his guru does not negate the rest of his actions, and thus when we judge a person, we must analyse their overall character and not come to a conclusion based on just one incident.

Q. 70

What decides the future of a special/intellectually disabled child since he cannot perform any karma?

Whatever happens to us is beyond our control. But how we respond is a choice. We begin our life from the point we left off in the previous one.

Whatever karma caused a child to be born with a disability, we should know that that particular karma is exhausted. The child has incurred that karma.

Whatever remaining karma of the child is left, positive and negative, will determine the starting point (where and how he is born etc) of that child in his next life since karmic cycle can continue for many lifetimes.

But we must also know that our future body and destination depend on the consciousness we cultivate

In such a situation, the parents can play an important role. They can encourage the spiritual growth of the child by providing devotional stimuli. Devotional stimuli can spiritualize the consciousness of the child. The child can be exposed to the sound of the devotional chanting of God's names, fame, qualities and pastimes from the holy scriptures. Further, the parents can pray for the child. Prayers done with sincere intention for someone's well-being are always answered.

While our actions in this life are shaped by our karma, what happens is also shaped by our circumstances. The child cannot do any karma, but the parents have a special opportunity here, to choose to give that child spiritual stimuli.

Either we can accept that in life, everything happens by chance and that we are just plain unlucky, or we can accept that there is a plan, but we are not always able to figure out what it is.

We should see that this child has come into our life to give us an opportunity to learn selfless love. When a parent loves a child, that parental love itself is selfless. But still, there is expectation; my child will grow up, my child will spread my fame. But this child will not do that for you. Also at the same time, we see that it is by God's arrangement that this child has come into our life. Every single thing that we do for this child, God accepts that service through this child.

The child may not have the free will to choose what to be conscious about, but if a spiritual environment is provided, the child can become spiritually conscious. And when the child becomes completely spiritually conscious, he gets liberated.

So sometimes bad things, in fact terrible things, can happen in our life. But if we have spiritual consciousness, we can minimize the agony that comes. We can find opportunity for that person's spiritual growth as well as our spiritual growth even in such an adverse situation.

Q. 71

Are dreams real or not?

Yes and no!

Srila Baladev Vidyabhushan, a prominent Vaishnava spiritual master who lived in the eighteenth century has said, 'In our dreams we are observers or participants, but we are not the controllers.'

Dreams are real in some senses. Some people are constantly distressed by disease, the loss of loved ones or a job and so on. All of us experience distress, but some people in some phases of their life face many problems. Why? There is a law of karma where for every action, there is a reaction. For the major karmas we do, reactions come on the physical level. We may suffer a fracture, lose a job or our loved one might abandon us. These are major reactions. But for minor karmas that we have done, we get reactions in dreams. So when we have a bad dream, that is also a reaction to a specific karma or a set of karmas. Thus, some people have good dreams and some have bad ones.

Dreams are also real in the sense that we do experience what comes in the dream; we experience pleasure and pain, and that is also a karmic reaction to what we have done in the past.

Nonetheless, dreams must never push us to live a life of paranoia. Some dreams may be prophecies of a sort, which may become real. Some of them may just be fantasies. Sometimes our fears in our conscious or subconscious mind lead to nightmares.

When we dream of something disturbing, we need not panic. We must simply remember the Supreme Lord Krishna by chanting His holy names:

Hare Krishna Hare Krishna Krishna Krishna Hare Hare
Hare Rama Hare Rama Rama Rama Hare Hare

This will drive away all types of inauspiciousness. In fact, the greatest of calamities can be warded off by the remembrance of the Lord.

Q. 72

Why do we shave our heads at Tirupati Balaji?

Tirupati is one of the holiest places in the world. Visiting holy places has been an important aspect of our culture, and countless pilgrims visit this holy site every year. They stand in queue for hours, dying to get a glimpse of the holy deity of Lord Vishnu even if for a few seconds.

Apart from getting blessed with the darshan of the Lord, they also shave their heads, which has long been a tradition.

The purpose of going on a pilgrimage to a holy place is to increase our attachment to the divine (God) and decrease our attachment to the mundane or matter. This is accomplished in two ways:

1. By visiting holy sites, having the darshan of the Lord, hearing and chanting the glories of the Lord, offering worship, giving charity etc.
2. By giving up things of personal sense gratification or things that are dear to us such as certain types of food, our hair etc.

Srimad Bhagavatam, while predicting the happenings of the Kali Yuga, mentions in the twelfth canto how people in this yuga would spend an enormous amount of time and energy in arranging and rearranging their hair in different fashions. We see this happening today as hair is considered to be a symbol of beauty.

People are very attached to their hair. So from the spiritual perspective, one way to detach ourselves is to not pay attention to our hair, in the manner of many saints, who allow their hair to grow long and become matted.

Another way is to shave off our hair as many sanyasis do.

Thus, the real spirit behind shaving the head is to demonstrate detachment to the material in front of the Lord by giving up something that is dear to us.

Since the hair is a symbol of beauty and adds to our ego, sacrificing it indicates that we are sacrificing our ego at the lotus feet of the Lord. It is a sign of humility—the foremost quality that touches the Lord's heart.

Also, everything belongs to God and everything is meant to be used in His service. Some things that we are attached to can be used directly in the Lord's service. For example, our wealth, which can be used to render direct service.

But there are certain things that we are attached to that are considered impure and thus cannot be offered in the Lord's service. Our hair is one such thing. Thus, we serve the Lord by giving up such things. Just as if a child wants to please his parents, one way is to offer them what will make them happy. But another way is to give up something that is bad.

However, today, most people shave their heads expecting their material desires to be fulfilled in return. The true spirit behind the shaving of one's head has been forgotten. Any ritual without the proper spirit is like an empty bullet—a lot of noise but no effect.

The essence behind the act is to decrease our attachment to the mundane by sacrificing that which takes our focus away from God. If we remain infatuated by our own selves, how will our hearts ever get attracted to the all-attractive Lord, the sole purpose for which we go to a holy place!

Q. 73

Why do spiritualists recommend food without onion and garlic?

'We are what we eat.'

Human life is special and meant for higher enquiry, i.e., seeking answers to questions like 'Who am I', 'What is the purpose of life', 'Who is God', etc. This applies to not just practicing spiritualists but to every human being.

To make higher enquiries we need to be in the mode of goodness. Mind and sense control, tolerance, discrimination, sticking to one's prescribed duty, truthfulness, mercy, satisfaction in any condition, generosity, renunciation of sense gratification, faith in the spiritual master, being embarrassed at improper action, charity, simplicity, humbleness and satisfaction within oneself are qualities of the mode of goodness. Our food plays a crucial role in achieving this.

Even on a material platform we can feel how when we are calmer we can handle situations better.

The Bhagavad Gita (17.7) talks about foods in various modes and the qualities associated with them:

aharas tv api sarvasya
tri-vidho bhavati priyaḥ

'Even the food each person prefers is of three kinds,
according to the three modes of material nature.'

Onion and garlic fall in the category of foods in the mode of
ignorance. When we eat food cooked with onion and garlic,
we also tend to get affected by the qualities associated with
the mode such as laziness, indolence, sleep, etc.

As Lord Krishna mentions in the Bhagavad Gita (14.8):

tamas tv ajnana-jam viddhi
mohanam sarva-dehinam
pramadalasya-nidrabhis
tan nibadhnati bharata

'O son of Bharata, the mode of ignorance causes the
delusion of all living entities. The result of this mode
is madness, indolence and sleep, which bind the
conditioned soul.'

Eating onion and garlic is not equivalent to eating non-
vegetarian food, but it certainly has an adverse effect on our
consciousness. It covers our intelligence, thus affecting our
decision-making abilities, especially when it comes to the
most crucial aspect of human life, which is self-realization and
God realization. Only when we are in the mode of goodness
can we truly appreciate and experience real peace and aspire

for real and eternal happiness, which comes from the spiritual platform.

Thus avoiding certain things as onion and garlic is not just a choice but becomes an absolute necessity when we understand the purpose behind such avoidance.

Q. 74

Does Lord Shiva smoke or consume marijuana/weed?

Srimad Bhagavatam (12.13.16) describes Lord Shiva's position;

nimna-ganam yatha ganga
devanam achyuto yatha
vaishnavanam yatha shambhuh
purananam idam tatha

'Just as the Ganga is the greatest of all rivers, Lord
Achyuta(Krishna) the supreme among deities and Lord
Śambhu [Shiva] the greatest of Vaishnavas, so Shrimad-
Bhagavatam is the greatest of all Puranas.'

So he is the greatest Vaishnava and sincere Vaishnavas strictly
avoid any kind of intoxication as a principle. So there is no
question of Lord Shiva smoking.

Further, there is not even a single reference to this regard in any of the scriptures.

This dubious idea is spread by those who themselves want to smoke and they use Lord Shivas's name to validate their addiction. This is called 'imitation'.

They say because Lord Shiva smokes, so they can also smoke.

And let us suppose for once we accept what these people say. But then why do they want to copy Lord Shiva in this regard only and not other aspects? Lord Shiva drank an entire ocean of poison, has snakes around his neck, moves around the crematoriums, smears ashes all over his body and lives on a mountain without a house. Why don't these people first show everyone that they can exhibit such extraordinary powers as well before they can spoil Shiva's name? The truth is that they cannot. They are just too addicted to something and very conveniently pass the buck to Lord Shiva saying, 'Since he does it, so can we!'

Those who want to smoke marijuana, justifying this by Shiva's smoking it, will first have to prove their prowess by drinking an ocean of poison without being harmed.

Last Words

Half knowledge is a dangerous thing. Whenever we come across some piece of information, we must fact-check before arriving at a conclusion.

The spread of misinformation is inherently human. The network effect of social media has broadened the sources of information and misinformation as well.

We tend not to look for what we do not see. We rather rely on the information that is directly available to us, without being fully aware of what we do not know. If we just see some elements of a story, we construct the best story we can out of those partial elements. Part of the approach of fact-checking is the awareness of the cognitive biases innate to each of us. While these biases help us navigate everyday life, they can cause us to overlook relevant facts, even when they are clearly presented.

Reality is more than the information we can perceive. It includes the availability of information from authentic sources, most powerful of which are the scriptures, the lawbooks for humankind, especially when it comes to questions about life and *its various aspects.*

Ask the Monk is about our journey from confusion to clarity, from darkness to light and from ignorance to enlightenment.

As Brihadaranyaka Upanishad, states:

asato ma sad gamaya, tamaso ma jyotir gamaya, mrityor ma amritam gamaya

'Lead us from ignorance to truth, from darkness to light, and from death to immortality.'

BIBLIOGRAPHY

Basham, A.L. *The Wonder That Was India: A Survey of the Culture of the Indian Sub-Continent Before the Coming of the Muslims.* London: Sidgwick & Jackson, 1954.

Costanza, Robert, d'Arge, Ralph and others. 'The Value of the world's Ecosystem services and natural capital'. *Nature.* 15 May 1997. https://www.esd.ornl.gov/benefits_conference/nature_paper.pdf.

Dasa, Purnaprajna. *Mahabharata.* The Bhaktivedanta Book Trust.

Narayana, M. *The Hitopadesa.* Penguin Classics, 2007.

Prabhupada, A.C. Bhaktivedanta Swami Srila. *Srimad Bhagavatam Set [Original First Edition 30 Volume] A Cultural Presentation for the Respiritualization of the World.* The Bhaktivedanta Book Trust, 1989.

Bhagavad Gita-As It Is. The Bhaktivedanta Book Trust, 1997.

Sri Isopanisad. The Bhaktivedanta Book Trust, 2011.

'Bhagavad Gita Lectures'. Prabhupada Books. https://prabhupadabooks.com/classes/bg/8/14-15/new_york/november/16/1966.

Sri Caitanya-caritamrta. The Bhaktivedanta Book Trust, 1974.

Sabom, Michael B. *Recollections of Death: A Medical Investigation*. USA: HarperCollins, 1981.

Stevenson, Dr Ian. *20 Cases Suggestive of Reincarnation*. University of Virginia Press, 1966.

Cases of the Reincarnation Type, Vol. I: Ten Cases in India. University of Virginia Press, 1975.

Cases of the Reincarnation Type, Vol. II: Ten Cases in Sri Lanka. University of Virginia Press, 1978.

Cases of the Reincarnation Type, Vol. III: Twelve Cases in Lebanon and Turkey. University of Virginia Press, 1980.

Cases of the Reincarnation Type, Vol. IV: Twelve Cases in Thailand and Burma. University of Virginia Press, 1983.

Children Who Remember Previous Lives: A Question of Reincarnation (Revised Edition). McFarland & Co Inc, 2000.

Where Reincarnation and Biology Intersect. Praeger Publishers, 1997.

European Cases of the Reincarnation Type. McFarland & Company, 2003.

Thakura, Bhaktivinoda, Maharaj, Bhaktivedanta Narayana. *Jaiva-Dharma: The essential function of the soul*. Gaudiya Vedanta Publications, 2002.

Thakura, Srila Bhaktisiddhanta Saraswati. *Sri Brahma Samhita*. The Bhaktivedanta Book Trust, 1990.

The Spiritual Scientist, 'Is there any proof of reincarnation?' *The Spiritual Scientist*. 15 October 2011. https://www. thespiritualscientist.com/2011/10/proof-of-reincarnation/.

Tucker, Jim B. *Life before Life: A Scientific Investigation of Children's Memories of Previous Lives*. USA: St. Martin's Griffin, 2008.

Vyasa, Krishna Dwaipayana, Vidyabhushan, Baladev. *Vedanta Sutra*. https://archive.org/stream/BaladevaVidyabhusana SriVedantaSutra/Baladeva_Vidyabhusana_Sri_Vedanta-sutra_djvu.txt.

Ward, Keith. *Is Religion Dangerous?*. London: Lion Hudson Plc, 2006.

Weiss, Dr Brian. *Many Lives, Many Masters: The True Story of a Prominent Psychiatrist, His Young Patient and the Past-life Therapy That Changed Both Their Lives*. United Kingdom: Piatkus, 1994.

World Health Organization, 'Suicide'. 17 June 2021. https://www.who.int/news-room/fact-sheets/detail/ suicide#:~:text=More%20than%20700%20000%20 people,15%2D19%20year%2Dolds.

World Health Organization, 'Obesity and overweight'. 9 June 2021. https://www.who.int/news-room/fact-sheets/ detail/obesity-and-overweight.

World Health Organization, 'As more go hungry and malnutrition persists, achieving Zero Hunger by 2030 in doubt, UN report warns'. 13 July 2020. https://www. who.int/news/item/13-07-2020-as-more-go-hungry-and-malnutrition-persists-achieving-zero-hunger-by-2030-in-doubt-un-report-warns.

Acknowledgements

I would like to express the eternal debt I owe to His Divine Grace A.C. Bhaktivedanta Swami Srila Prabhupada (Founder Acharya of ISKCON), who always inspired, trained and encouraged his followers to enquire about the absolute truth.

My sincere gratitude to His Holiness Radhanath Swami Maharaj, my spiritual master, who, over the years, through his words, has solidified the understanding reflected in the pages of this book.

I cannot thank enough, Chaitanya Charan Prabhu for his on-going series of Q & A (thespiritualscientist.com). His answers provided a lot of clarity on many intricate subjects.

Many thanks are due to Resham Mehta and Sneha Makhija for helping me in putting the content of this book together.

I fall short of words as I begin to thank Gurveen Chadha and the team at Penguin who went out of their way and agreed to publish this book in a record time. They were extremely kind and quick for which I will remain eternally grateful to them. May Lord Krishna showers His choicest blessing upon all of them.

One person who has been a strong support right from the beginning and extremely enthusiastic in my every project is Dipti Patel (wordfamous.in). I thank her immensely for connecting me with the team at Penguin, after which everything fell in place.

Lastly, I wish to thank all my friends, across all age groups, who through their constant queries and interactions over the years, inspired a need to come out with a book like this.

Thanks for being a part of this sacred journey.

Happy reading!